The Strategy MindSet 2.0

The Strategy Mindset 2.0:

A Practical Guide to the Design
And Implementation of Strategy

Dr. Chuck Bamford

ISBN: 9781088768402

Table of Contents

Introduction

Organizations survive (and hopefully thrive) because they are able to change. No matter how successful the business has been, its future lies in the ability to attain real returns from its competitive advantages. This can only be accomplished by staying well ahead of competitor moves intended to encroach on those advantages as well as continually designing and implementing new competitive advantages.

Strategy is the process of developing and implementing *real* competitive advantages such that customers will go past your competitors and buy from you at a price that allows for substantial economic (or social, in some cases) returns.

There are many strategy books on the market. Some are textbooks that are really designed as supports to classroom lectures and aids for the uninitiated to the basics of strategy and how it is employed at the executive level. For the practical business executive, they are thick, mind-numbing reads (because they are not meant to be read like a book) that are five-hundred-plus pages of text with thousands of citations and a $200-plus price point. I know; I've written a few, and one of my big strategy textbooks is currently headed to its 16th edition (*Concepts in Strategic Management and Business Policy*, Pearson).

There are also so-called strategy books written by famous CEOs who try to share the wisdom they think they found while running a particular organization. Some of these books provide an interesting insight into history, but only a rare few (and they are remarkable) provide any clue to the application of strategy at another organization in another time and place. Most are simply stories. Stories are nice for context, but without real frameworks that have been proven to work in many contexts, they are just fun reads with a practical value near zero.

Then there are a vast array of books written by people with little or no real understanding of strategy who have decided to anoint themselves with titles like "strategy consultant," "thought leader" (a title I find particularly ridiculous), "strategy guru," or my favorite, "game changer." They share their lightweight insight often with ridiculous titles in an effort to gain some notoriety, speaking contracts, and press. They spell out a vague multistep approach (putting it in terms of numbers seems to be in vogue, like "Ten Things" or "Eight Paths") that they are sure will work and try to develop a cult following of their preaching. I've read many of these in a vain attempt to keep ahead of graduate students and executives asking me if I've read this or that book. They have universally been a waste of time. Without the combination of real research that looks at hundreds of organizations and a solid foundation in practical applications across many industries, all you are left with is another story (and substantial frustration as you try to apply their eight whatever's). Unfortunately, I have watched (and in some cases been involved in the cleanup) as some senior leader at an organization reads one of these and decides that it is *the path* for their organization. They require everyone to read the book and bring the author in to completely confuse the organization with their "pop" approach to strategy. They are fiction. They look good, they sound good, and they may even seem to make some sense; however, they are dangerous for your business.

In February 2015 *The Strategy Mindset* was published as a simple yet practical guide to creating business strategy using well-researched, practical, and battle-tested processes. The goal was to establish the fundamentals of the design and implementation processes of strategy in a readable and easily accessible format. The approaches used in that book and in this second edition are the gold standard for developing and executing real competitive advantages such that customers will go past your competitors and come to you because you have those advantages.

The big changes (and the reason for a 2nd edition) include the following:

1. The addition of several elements of strategy design and implementation that were not included in the first edition for brevity. It has become clear in my work over the past four years that these topics need to be addressed. These include discussions of industry types as well as methods for classifying and analyzing competitors.

2. Updating and adding new examples used in the book.

3. Adding a section on vision statements, establishing values and principles, including their design and use.

4. Adding in new examples (along with some analysis) of great and awful mission/vision statements.

5. Updating the design and use of the one-page strategy map. Research into its practical application has substantially changed the elements in a good strategy map. I have updated and included a number of new example maps.

6. The whole approach to determining the perfect customer for an organization has been significantly refined. This includes approaches for locating these "perfect customers" and increasing your sales success rate.

7. Significantly more information about the design and practical use of project plans to implement strategy.

8. A section specifically focused on the unique issues related to nonprofits.

   Strategy is a process that, at its core, consists of designing and implementing elements of the organization that will draw customers past your competitors, allow you to charge more than your competitors, and/or provide you with a cost advantage.

Despite all the rhetoric, your people are *not* a competitive advantage (they are how you deliver on your competitive advantages), quality is generally too generic to be one (most customers can't objectively determine quality differences), customer service is simply table stakes for virtually every organization (every organization claims that customers are their first priority), and releasing yet another variation of your product line just adds complexity and costs but is only *very rarely* part of a competitive advantage. Customers hear this same jargon from all your competitors. A successful strategy starts and ends with the customer you are trying to convince to buy from you. They don't only look at your offering and are rarely persuaded by false claims.

Despite decades of research, *businesses are still terrible at strategy*! Executives don't understand it. They think it is some type of pure art or gut feelings with which one proves one's manhood/womanhood, or they simply throw up their hands and surrender to SWOT (Strengths, Weaknesses, Opportunities & Threats)! Please, if you get nothing else from this book, or if you read this opening and decide not to read any further, do one thing for your organization—*never* use SWOT as a strategy approach again. That alone should help the bottom line.

Strategy has most of its written roots in Sun Tzu's *The Art of War* and a long history of military application that was loosely translated into business. Those crude translations worked well while the logistic ability to reach new customers was expanding rapidly, conglomerates were seen as the epitome of effectiveness, and organization growth was virtually assured in a rapidly growing economy.

All of that started falling apart in the 1970s. It was probably falling apart before then, but the fallout from the OPEC-driven energy embargos, the ending of the Vietnam War, and the introduction of the personal computer meant that strategy no longer followed the command-and-control, conquer-and-succeed strategy models that had been in vogue for so long. A famous line used over and over was that soldiers (and businesspeople) prior to that era were trained to kill anything that came over the hill, not nimbly assess changing conditions and shoot judiciously.

A winning business strategy must focus on why customers *really* buy a product or service from an organization and what distinguishes that purchase in the eye of the customer. Strategy has to be designed and crafted for the real needs and wants of specific customer groups.

Business strategy is at best 50 percent science and 50 percent art. It is probably more like 35 percent science and 65 percent art, but there is a science. There is a process that works. If done with some rigor, applying the science of strategy will separate your organization from all of your competitors and allow you to earn extraordinary returns. It must regularly be reviewed and potentially refreshed as conditions change in the market. Your competitive advantages can (and over some period of time most likely will) be taken away by competitors, but it is essential that you develop a strategy if you wish to drive for consistent performance above the median relative to your competitors.

I don't say this lightly. As a corporate guy in the 1980s and early 1990s, I was continually frustrated with our organization's inability to move beyond the superficial talk about how our employees were our competitive advantage or how our dedication to quality, Kaizen (continuous improvement approach), customer service, or any of the other pop approaches of the day would lead to extraordinary returns. As I pursued my PhD, I was astounded to find out that many of the approaches we used were well understood to be useless. Why don't executives know this?

In general, customers could care less whom you employ as long as the organization delivers on what it promises. Customers are indifferent to your efficiency; they know that every organization claims that quality is job number one, and they are immune to the preaching about how the customer is the centerpiece of the organization. Unless you can visibly show the customer that they will be treated substantially differently from your competitors, they already know that customer service is not the centerpiece of your strategy!

Actually, these are all well-intentioned and, in most cases, totally believed approaches (at least at the executive level). I will discuss many of these myths in the first chapter (including the belief that SWOT is somehow an analysis tool). The rest of this book will take you through the processes you need to design and implement a real strategy in your organization. Strategy is not tactics, and while it must translate into operational efforts, it is not an operational plan. You already know how to run the fundamentals, yet half of strategy is ensuring that you are not frustrating customers or employees.

Strategy is not easy, but it can be done quickly (if senior management is truly motivated), and it will have a profound impact on your organization. I have had the opportunity to be a part of many organizations that have gone through the processes detailed in this book. Good strategy is industry agnostic. It works in manufacturing, services, nonprofits, trade associations, and even governmental organizations (albeit with quite the nuances). Once all of the employees understand where we will focus our efforts, what we would like to hear customers (and perhaps competitors, community leaders, and stakeholders) say about our competitive advantages, and how we will measure that effort, we get tens of thousands of decisions each day all headed in the roughly the same direction. At some point, the customers see the consistency (because consistency is the hallmark of a good strategy implementation), and it begins to feel like the whole organization is running down a hill—except with money!

I am a student, researcher, developer, teacher, and practitioner of strategy. I helped pioneer both the design and business application of this *practical strategy approach*.

I've used this approach for the past twenty-five plus years with hundreds of organizations and have taught this approach to tens of thousands as a:

1. consultant and founder of a strategy consulting firm based in Raleigh, NC,

2. author of five textbooks (including the market-leading strategy textbook at Pearson, 15th edition, and entrepreneurship textbook at McGraw-Hill, 3rd edition),

3. author of *eighteen* research articles, including some of the top-referred academic journals in the fields of strategy and entrepreneurship, and

4. professor at Duke University, University of Notre Dame, University of Richmond, Texas Christian University, and Tulane University, among others, where I have been awarded twenty-two individual teaching awards.

I hope you enjoy this fast-paced look at a complex subject. The concepts are not that difficult to understand. Mastery in application will take time. I have embedded examples and short stories while trying not to distract from the message. Therefore, this is a short book (in the world of strategy) meant to be used as a guide to actually getting this done at your organization. There are many more nuances to all the approaches discussed in this book; however, they are for the hearty who want to dig deep in the subject.

I encourage you to write me with your feedback, thoughts, stories, and advice. Every organization is unique, but the approaches in this book are battle tested, grounded in solid theory, and they employ a modified version of the latest approaches in the field today. I modified this approach many years ago to account for the realities of business as opposed to the purest, most theoretical take on the subject. By no means will this book answer all your questions, but there is enough here for you to get to work.

Chuck Bamford, PhD
@DrChuckBamford
www.bamfordassociates.com
cbamford@bamfordassociates.com

Chapter 1

You Must Be Kidding!
(Or, We Need to Get Rid of the Myths Before We Can Apply Real Strategy)

Before the executives of any organization can begin to develop a real strategy (that is, something that actually separates your product/service/offering from your competitors' such that customers will bypass your competitors and come to you), they have to get their people to abandon the myths that muddy the message. As with most myths, they are grounded in history, are easy to understand, and have some face validity.

If you can't accept that some of these myths exist and might be holding back your organization, then there is no need to read on. Take the blue pill (think *The Matrix*, Morpheus, and a conversation with Neo in the rain), and go back to the world where it will all be OK. You can do SWOT, be convinced that you just simply have better people, and keep adding SKUs in an effort to grow sales (but not profit).

I say this only somewhat tongue in cheek. Holding on to myths inhibits your ability to develop real strategy and, more importantly, will virtually prevent you from convincing your employees to implement something that allows the organization to win over customers.

Letting go of myths can be a painful process—somewhat like an exorcism—but I'll try to give you enough information here to explain why each must be let go (you will no doubt have to contend with employees who will disagree). I could write a separate book on many of these topics with countless examples, but I've tried to keep this concise for your reading pleasure.

1

Myth 1: My People Are My Competitive Advantage

This is one of the favorite responses when I ask executives to describe their strategy or even just one competitive advantage. It is certainly the most politically correct statement that one can make, and if the same executives said that employees are generally interchangeable, they would be accused of...well, being out of touch with what matters in an organization.

The moment that you actually believe that your employees are better, smarter, and friendlier than your competitors' is the moment that your competitors will start beating you in the market. You have the same (or relatively the same) collection of amazing employees, good employees, capable employees, poor employees, and employees who should have been let go a long time ago. All the HR processes in the world today have not changed that dynamic in companies. The employees you have working in your organization are a combination of *luck* (the biggest factor), HR practices, networking, referrals, and did I mention *luck*?

"My people are my competitive advantage" (always said with pride).

"Of course they are; none of the competitors have people!"

"Well, our people are better" (spoken somewhat defensively).

"Sure they are!"

Employees are *not* your competitive advantage—they are how you deliver your competitive advantages. Their actions and efforts are critical to that delivery, but (for the most part) the actual person doing the delivery is *not* the competitive advantage. I'm not trying to be divisive here, but most of your customers do not generally care who takes care of their business needs as long as the needs are taken care of.

If you lose an employee (even one loved by your customers), you do not go out of business; you replace them and move on.

This general view does not apply to every employee in an organization, just most. At every organization I have ever worked with or for, there is a contingent of "franchise" employees. Those are employees who, if they left the organization, would impact the success of that organization quite substantially. We all know who these folks are, and if executives are smart, they take care of these employees to ensure that they stay with the organization. These franchise employees are not just the customer-facing employees, nor are they exclusively at the top of the house; they reside throughout an organization.

How many franchise employees do you need? As many (relatively) as your competitors have. Some seem to believe that a whole organization built on these types of people would perform better, but the costs of doing so can be substantial both financially and in terms of your ability to get basic work done at your organization. If your competitors have ten franchise employees, then you probably need to be relatively close to ten as well. Fewer will impact your ability to deliver at least an equivalent experience to the customer as that provided by your competitors. More has the tendency to increase your costs and ability to move quickly.

That said, virtually every other employee is relatively interchangeable (including executive management team members—actually, *often* executive management team members). The most fundamental reason for this is the customer experience. The customer is buying from your organization for a small set of promises that your organization pitches as the reason for customers to bypass competitors and buy from your organization. In most instances, the employee is the conduit that delivers on those promises.

- If you walk into the bank to make a deposit, and your favorite teller is not there, you don't walk out in a huff—you make the deposit. Most customers would not even be able to tell you what the teller does; they just know that money goes into their account.

- If you walk into a fast-food restaurant to get a meal, you are indifferent as to who makes the meal or hands it to you. You have chosen that particular restaurant because of the implied "promises" that have led to you bypassing competitors for that company's offering. For example, if you buy into the pitch that employees at Chick-fil-A are "nicer" (they say thanks, ask what they can do for you, provide you with refills at your table, etc.), then it is the system in place that makes those actions a consistent part of the performance you expect. It is not the particular employee that is the advantage; it is what they deliver on a consistent basis.

- When your new Amazon Echo arrives, do you care who built it, packaged it, and delivered it? Unlikely. You have acquired it over the competitor offerings because of a set of promises made by Amazon about what you can do with it in your home.

- If your power goes out, you don't care who the technician is that turns it back on; you just want the power back on. You presume that the power organization has employed well-trained personnel who will bring the power back on as quickly as is reasonably possible.

- If you call a cruise line to book a trip, you don't really care who is on the other end as long as he or she is competent (friendly is a bonus). You chose that particular cruise line for the variety of promises that it makes about the experience you will have during your trip.

- If you order a new part from a manufacturer, you don't care which employee makes it; you just want the part. You bought the part without any idea of who in the organization was responsible for making it, shipping it, billing for it, etc. The performance of each of those employees can make the experience better or worse (in some cases so much worse that you will no longer do business with the organization), but it is not the *why* of your decision to do business with that organization.

- Do you have any idea who the pilot was or what qualifications the crew had on your last flight? No, because it doesn't matter to you as the customer, and it had no influence at all in your decision to buy a ticket. One of those pilots was a true franchise player (not a competitive advantage) for a short period of time, were you fortunate enough to have Captain Sully Sullenberger (but you did not know if he would captain your plane when you bought the ticket). Unfortunately for all of us, he is retired now. You expect the pilot and copilot (and for that matter, the whole crew) to be trained on that particular airframe, competent, and sober (personally, I find that a little prayer goes a long way before a flight, but that is a different issue). Even if the pilot was someone you recognized when you heard the announcement, you did not buy the ticket to get that pilot—it was simply luck of the draw.

This logic can be applied to most employees at most companies in most industries. I've seen it in practice with law firms, where the client may follow the departing attorney or may not; in consulting practices, where the organization has a long-term relationship with a firm and is sorry to see that particular consultant, manager, or partner go; in auto dealerships, insurance companies, manufacturing businesses, associations, nonprofits, banks, and virtually all retail operations—you get the picture. B2B or B2C makes no difference.[1]

I talked with a bank executive once who simply insisted that his bank's competitive advantage was its people. I asked him where he got his people. Of course, he got them from other banks, university recruiting, job postings, referrals, and luck (much like all their competitors). He insisted that he only hired good employees, and I resisted the desire to ask him if he had ever managed employees that he thought should be fired or if any employees were ever rated below average (perhaps the organization was in Lake Wobegon).

I asked him what he thought the CEO of Bank Y (one of his competitors) would say about their own employees.

Might it be something like, "Well, we wish we could say that our employees were our competitive advantage, but unfortunately, all the good ones are at X, so all we are left with over here is crap. We just try to do our best with crap employees".

No! *Of course not.* They would both say it is their people and both would be *wrong!*

This is simply a black hole in strategy. If you are convinced that somehow you have better employees than your competitors, then you distort your business practices to try and take advantage of that aspect. Picture the commercials, websites, and marketing materials that constantly pitch that the difference in their business is the people who work for the business.

---

1   Business to Business (B2B) and Business to Consumer (B2C)

Enormous efforts are put into recruitment, employee engagement practices, benefits, opportunities for personal and professional growth, pinball machines, snack carts, and virtually every silly thing you see some companies do to try and make employees feel the "love" at work. Customers don't buy from you because you do this, and you don't end up with "better" employees.

There is more than enough research available (despite the hordes of books written on the subject trying to get you to do more for your employees) to show that these approaches have little (far below their cost) or no impact on turnover, productivity, or consistency in handling customers.

Customers do not buy from Walmart because Suzie works there. Despite all the great press about how Costco treats their employees, customers are indifferent as to who checks them out of the store. Customers do not get their car washed by a particular business because Bill works there, and they do not deposit their money with Bank of America because Ralph works there. Customers expect employees to be competent, relatively accommodating, and accountable (as I said earlier, we'll go with friendly as a bonus).

Interestingly, the other argument relates to the ability to recruit and retain employees. You must be at the median level of engagement, opportunities, and perks for employees. If your competitors raise the stakes, then you must at least match the median expectation in your industry in order to be able to draw from the same relative set of potential employees. I've watched as the length of maternity/paternity leave has grown in the consulting industry. The companies were generally reluctant to offer this perk but have been forced to continually increase the offering as boutique firms drove the increases and were able to out-recruit competitors.

We need our employees to do their jobs and do those jobs well, but that is *table stakes* in an industry and is expected out of every competitor. Beyond that, customers are choosing to do business with your organization for other reasons. Those reasons will enable you to charge more and may lead to being an organization of choice for customers. This is why we have to figure out what those elements are and how to focus as much time, money, and mental firepower as we can on those elements.

Employees are *not* your competitive advantage.

Myth 2: SWOT Analysis Will Allow Us to Develop a Strategy

SWOT (as applied to the business world) is generally viewed as a creation of the 1970s, when business strategy was really business policy. When I took business policy as an undergraduate student, we read cases to "learn" what to do in business (sadly, some professors still think this is all there is to strategy). There was very little content knowledge to share about how to design or execute strategy outside of a military model. Once in business, we were expected to use corporate history, experience or examples in the press as a foundation for what passed as our strategic thinking.

SWOT was an attempt to bring some structure to the topic, and as a conceptual approach, it is still fairly robust. Unfortunately, many authors, academics, and practitioners decided that SWOT was an *analysis* tool and a means for an organization to develop its strategy instead of recognizing that it is an effective way to present aspects of an organization.

SWOT is *not* **strategy, and it is** *not* **an analysis tool**. Unless you are simply using it as a team-building exercise (and even then, I would suggest that there are many far better approaches to use), taking five minutes to do a SWOT exercise is a five-minute waste of time at an organization.

More money has been wasted on SWOT than virtually any other aspect of thought in business.

For those of you fortunate enough to not know yet, SWOT is an acronym for a two-by-two approach with four quadrants consisting of Strengths, Weaknesses, Opportunities, and Threats. Anyone can create a SWOT chart. It is grounded in your own biases and view of the world. In the end, a completed SWOT chart is simply the opinion of the person or group filling it out. Companies over the years have dedicated untold dollars to meetings where groups throughout the organization craft a SWOT chart for their organization, their division, their product, etc. Then (of course) they emphasize their strengths, minimize their weaknesses, look for opportunities, and prepare for threats. It all sounds good. However, how do we decide which element falls into which box?

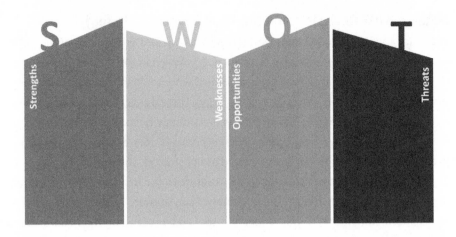

Just because someone believes X is a strength does not make it so. Attempting to use a SWOT approach is an inherently static look at the business based on a gut opinion of where everything is now. Furthermore, everything that is a strength is also a weakness. By the same token, everything that is an opportunity is also potentially a threat. Occasionally, one element can easily and correctly (based on the simplistic concepts) fit into all four quadrants. This approach to strategy design was abandoned by most serious strategy practitioners in the late 1990s for these and a whole host of other reasons.[2]

Just for fun, over the years I asked each of my then eight-year-old sons to do a SWOT of his third-grade class. I taught each of them the technique in about three minutes. The fact that an eight-year-old can learn it effectively in three minutes should tell you everything you need to know about SWOT as tool for crafting million- or billion-dollar decisions. It should also tell you that any consulting organization or organization executive who suggests this should be run out of your office.

I then asked his teacher and his principal to each do one. All of them had used SWOT in the past and felt like this would be a fun exercise. Not surprisingly, both times none of the three aligned at all. None of them had even one of the same items in the strengths box (meaning that leadership from the principal was not very well defined). In the hierarchy of the school whose take on this should be used? We would generally

---

2   T. Hill and R. Westbrook, "SWOT Analysis: It's Time for a Product Recall," *Long Range Planning*, 30, no. 1 (February 1997): 46–52.

assume it should be the principal. So, if we are going to use such a blatantly opinion-based approach, we might as well just ask the principal to fill it out and tell everyone what it should be, then craft metrics and activities to reinforce that view.

Interestingly, my sons thought that recess and lunch were the strengths of third grade. Each boy also listed his teacher as a strength (albeit below the other two items), a weakness (there were always better teachers that they wished they had), an opportunity (for a variety of perks), and a threat (at the top for obvious reasons). I know it comes as a shock, but neither the teacher nor the principal listed recess or lunch as strengths.

There are volumes of material on the internet for you to read about the drawbacks of SWOT as an analysis tool. As I stated above, this approach was abandoned by most serious strategy practitioners more than two and a half decades ago, and yet I see it every year as I work with companies. Its staying power is mostly attributable to its ease of understanding, the feeling that something has been accomplished, and to the many, many non-strategy-trained professors at universities who "teach" it as a technique.

Serious practitioners of SWOT craft elaborate charts that have a vast list of elements in each of the four boxes. Your view of the organization will affect what you believe belongs in each category. Without some science as to what truly belongs in each box, all you have is opinion. However, as I pointed out at the beginning of this piece, SWOT is a fairly robust conceptual and effective presentation approach. If you look at each element, the fact is that you do want to know what would populate each of the four blocks; you just need to use a more precise and well-grounded approach for getting to each of these.

Do you want to know the strengths of your organization? Of course you do. There are well-honed techniques available for getting at the true strengths (differentiators) of your organization. It is only a strength if it helps separate your business from your competitors in the eyes of the customer. Understanding how to craft these advantages is one of the core goals of this book. Applying these tools will allow you to get a lot closer to a great strategy. Don't let anyone fool you; even with this, strategy is still mostly *art*!

Do you want to know the weaknesses of your organization? Of course you do. These are the standard elements of the business (the table stakes from the point of view of customers) being executed well below the median expectations in the industry. Something is a critical weakness if it impacts your ability to make a sale or a repeat sale. It is also a weakness if it prevents you from recruiting and/or retaining employees. Half of strategy design is identifying these critical weaknesses and putting a plan together to bring those elements up to the median expectation in your industry. Learning how to identify and address these weaknesses is also one of the core goals of this book.

Do you want to know the opportunities for your organization? Of course you do. However, something is only an opportunity if you have or will be able to develop a real competitive advantage that can be applied to this area and if the many external factor paths in a business operation can be understood. We utilize the same resource-based analysis approach in order to evaluate potential competitive advantages of the organization.

Do you want to know the threats to your organization? Of course you do. However, threats affect most companies in your industry. Therefore, there are a number of approaches to discern what these might be and how an organization can navigate them ahead of its competitors. A deep industry analysis provides significant insights that an organization's leadership can and should use. This is examined at length in this book.

What does this mean? It means that it is time to put SWOT to bed as a strategy analysis approach. After using some real science to discern competitive advantages, real competitive disadvantages, and future competitive market moves, if you wish to put all that into the SWOT boxes for a visual, you will achieve what was originally proposed as its best use.

Don't do SWOT!

Myth 3: The Product Life Cycle Will Help Me Decide on a Strategy

The product life cycle (PLC) most certainly exists, and it is quite fascinating to look back at the patterns over time with virtually every product or service. In general, we see a start with some form of introduction followed by a move through growth to maturity, and eventually, it either becomes a commodity (which really means that the rest of the competitors finally caught up, and there is some level of steady sales) or proceeds to some form of slow death. If you follow the logic of the observations, you realize that some products, services, and even whole businesses (think McDonald's) stay in a perpetual flatline maturity phase that fluctuates plus or minus around the general movements of the economy. Others are "reborn," giving the whole product line a newer lease on life (think iPhone 15 or the ten-blade razor).

It is interesting to note all the effort put into trying to figure out where in the life cycle a particular product or service is at a specific time. The theory of some marketing folks is that if you know where you are in the life cycle, then you know how to invest your resources.

From a strategy perspective, all of that would be fine if we had any idea where we were in the life cycle while we were actually in it and what the curve actually looks like—which we *cannot know as it is occurring*. No one can tell you with any precision where the HP Pavilion laptop, Samsung Galaxy phone, LG 4K television, or Hardees Frisco Thickburger is at the current time. It gets even more muddled when we look at a whole organization. Is each slight update to the product a new introduction, and what would that mean for our strategy decisions? Strategy is about the future of the organization.

Ask ten people to identify where the Cadillac is on the PLC, and you will get ten locations, each of which is just as reasonable as any of the others. In other words, despite all the statistical efforts to precisely locate the position on the curve, it is simply a guess. Unfortunately, this guess has significant resource implications for the business if it is believed.

Once an organization decides that X product or service is in the growth stage, then the organization is supposed to invest heavily. If it is in the maturity stage, then investments are to be cut back and the money generated used as a "cash cow." According to the textbooks on this subject, there are a vast array of moves that should be made during each stage. Every single product or service also has a unique curve (which, for obvious reasons, you would not know until well past when it happened). That is, the slope/variation of that curve is different for every product/service (traditionally using sales as the vertical axis and time as the horizontal axis); therefore, the concept of PLC cannot be applied in real time.

You know where you are in the life cycle only long after the product or service has ceased to be of practical value. PLC works very well as a historical observation and is simply useless as a tool for understanding current or future strategic approaches.

Strategy is about making decisions that will impact the success of the organization in the future. Those decisions must be made in the present, with information that is of value in the present. We simply do not know where we are in the PLC (nor what that curve will look like) until long after it has happened; therefore, it is *not* a technique that assists the design of strategy and is a waste of time, money, and effort.

Strategists don't waste time on the PLC!

Myth 4: We Shouldn't Look at What Competitors Are Doing—Let's Focus on What We Do

Here's one that somehow made it into the lore of exceptional business leadership that is completely counter to good strategy design. If you follow some of the interviews that have been broadcast over the years, you will find some leaders who insist that they pay no attention to competitors, as though that somehow made their organizations' performance more impressive.

It is hard to find a way to support this approach even at face value when we know that customers compare any product or service offered (whether B2B or B2C) to other alternatives. While we may (and hopefully do) have a core group of dedicated, loyal customers who will never consider the competition, this group of "perfect customers" is rarely big enough to allow a business to thrive.

Customers compare every offering, every product, and every aspect of a business not only to your direct competitors but also to other means of achieving a similar outcome.

An individual customer who has a car headlight out has a lot of possible solutions available. He or she can buy a bulb at any of the national auto parts chains (Advanced Auto, AutoZone, Napa, Pep Boys, etc.) if planning to change it at home. The same individual could go to any national chain or local mechanic to have it done, go to the dealership, or simply not replace the thing. All of these are options to the customer, and each one gets weighed based on the customer's own bounded rational approach.

When the offering by the competition/alternatives exceeds some internal threshold with the customer, that person is no longer our customer. I am continuously struck by the lack of knowledge of competitors and their offerings. Assumptions are made that have a dramatic impact on the positioning of products and services. Furthermore, competitors raise the bar continuously such that what you thought would be an advantage has already been taken away.

A classic example of this kind of ridiculous statement was reported on by the *Wall Street Journal* in June 2019. Discussing delivery approaches and why customers should choose Amazon, spokesperson Julie Law was reported to have said, "We don't put a lot of time and energy or focus into competitors because it can be distracting to being innovative for customers. We believe what we are offering to Prime members today is unmatched." The mere thought that one should not know this or that an organization could be innovative (whatever that word really means) without knowing whether another organization had already "innovated" something is absurd![3] Belief is not a competitive strategy.

We simply *must* know what our competitors are doing, how they are doing it, and how that might impact our sales. A deep understanding of competitors is actually *the* first step in developing a strategy. Trying to craft a strategy in isolation may feel comforting at the time, but you do a huge disservice to your organization when you don't run the organization from the perspective that your customers use to make decisions. What competitors do matters!

Know your competitors!

---

3   S. Herrera, "In Amazon vs. Walmart Delivery Battle, a Fresh Salvo," *Wall Street Journal*, June 4, 2019, https://www.msn.com/en-us/money/companies/in-amazon-vs-walmart-delivery-battle-a-fresh-salvo/ar-AACk522.

Myth 5: Quality or Customer Service Will Be Our Strategic Advantage

Customers certainly care about quality. That is to say, customers expect to receive slightly better quality than they hoped for when they bought the product or service from your organization. Most customers assume that quality is built into the point that the product or service performs as or slightly better than expected. Most customers have no idea what constitutes "quality" or how to truly evaluate it. It is a mantra in business that quality is the cornerstone of customer choice. It is not always or even generally true. By the way, customers (B2B or B2C) will certainly tell you that quality is an issue in their purchases; it is just not what separates one organization from the next—at least not *actual* quality.

When you put your strategy stake in the ground and claim that you are the quality choice for customers, you have put yourself in the position of proving it to customers in terms that customers care about and can actually judge for themselves. In general, this means that you have to be so far above the rest of the industry that it is obvious to customers. Anything short of this and the competitors can easily negate your so-called competitive advantage. Be very wary of this seductive approach.

Interestingly, you can use quality as a competitive advantage as long as you are able to get underneath this huge conceptual term. What specific elements of your product/service/offering can you list as being substantially better than competitors, *and* does it matter to your customer? Be specific, be able to back up your claims, be diligent about what the competitors are actually offering, and be rigorous about consistency within your organization. Make it real for customers, and you can use this as a potential competitive advantage. Make it generic, and customers just hear white noise.

The other big mantra is the focus on so-called customer service. It is shocking how many companies seem to truly believe that their strategy revolves around customer service. "It is what differentiates us in the market!" The drumbeat of customer service as our strategic differentiator is used by virtually every organization that I deal with in my consulting business. While it is certainly politically correct, this one is so far from being true that it is laughable.

Now let's be clear—it would be wonderful if overall customer service were really the cornerstone of a business. The entire business would be focused on the specific needs of the customer at that moment in time. Each customer would feel that they were truly important to the organization. The customer would bypass your competitors in order to feel special or feel that their purchase was truly appreciated. B2B customers would bypass competitors because they would feel that their needs were being fully supported in the moment.

When was the last time you felt that way at your bank, gas station, cleaner's, utility, fast-food restaurant, lawyer, doctor, university, or other organization? The answer is not much and, most importantly, not consistently.

A basic tenet of strategy is that whatever constitutes the elements of your competitive advantages must be consistently delivered to the customer. Instead, despite all the investment, talk, and management firepower aimed at improving customer service, the reality on the ground is as follows:

- **"We are unable refund your money."**

  - Are you kidding me? Give your money back to you?

- **"Our systems don't allow us to do that."**

  - They were designed in a patchwork system by IT folks who don't deal with customers, and anything special I do for you will cost me.

- **"You need to provide us with all of the details, including ticket number and record locators."**

  - Prove it. We hope you just go away.

- **"I know we said that, but..."**

  - Hey, sometimes we'll say anything to get you to buy.

- **"That is the way we handle all customers; you are not being treated unfairly."**

  - Sucky is as sucky does, and we do sucky really well.

- **"I wish we could do that, but..."**

  - It is not my fault that we won't accommodate you.

- **"Could I put you on hold?"**

  - Not really a question. This really means I'll get back to you when I'm ready.

- **"Please explain your reasoning in detail."**

  - We expect the customer to be our quality control.

- **"The manager should be back shortly."**

  - You are clearly asking for special treatment, and that will cost you a lot of time!

I'm sure you can add many more quotes to the refrain of "the customer is *not* the most important element in our business" mantra, and therefore customer service is not one of our competitive differentiators.

For the *vast* majority of companies, customer service is just table stakes. It is one of those areas where the organization needs to be within a reasonable distance of the average for the industry (actually measured as the median by strategists). Some industries have a very high median level of expected customer service primarily because the customers have a wide choice of options (e.g., four-star restaurants). Others are simply abysmal because they can get most of the business, they need without making any effort toward customer satisfaction (e.g., airlines, cable companies, government agencies).

A lot of money spent beefing up what passes for customer service is only of value if the organization can achieve a level of service so far above the competitors that customers truly notice the difference. This generally means that we again need to get underneath this concept and be very specific as to what constitutes something remarkable for customers. Perhaps we respond to all inquiries within a specific period of time that is game-changing in our industry, provide access to status information unknown in our industry, or can deliver at a guaranteed time when our competitors cannot. For customer service to have any value, it must be specific, measurable, proven, consistent, and something that matters to customers.

Otherwise, it is a waste of time, money, and resources to do much more than what is minimally expected in your industry. In other words, customer service is only rarely a strategy; mostly it consists of empty words into which companies pour money.

Be very wary of quality or customer service as a strategy!

Myth 6: We Are the Low-Cost Leader, or Let's Just Talk About Revenue

Virtually every organization at some point in its existence has had an executive convince the senior leadership team that cost cutting is a strategy. Top lines are not growing as hoped, competition is getting tougher, and most important to the executive team, bonuses are being cut. Executives are convinced that the organization can attain a competitive advantage by making Herculean efforts to lower costs (or at least earn their bonuses in the short run—probably the real reason).

Interestingly enough, this is absolutely true—for *one* organization in your competitive set, and the cost difference has to be substantial to be of any value. While cost containment is generally advisable as a tactic (as long as it does not impact the strategy being pursued by the organization), only one organization in any particular industry can actually be the low-cost leader. Everyone else is simply a wannabe without the ability to attain the same basis-point margins as the low-cost leader. The true low-cost leader can lower prices to the point where competitors are simply not profitable, while still maintaining healthy margins.

To truly be the low-cost leader is an all-encompassing strategy effort that requires the investment of time, effort, resources, and mental firepower to continuously drive costs from the business. It will only help the bottom line if one or more of the following occurs:

1. Your business is truly the low-cost leader, and that differential is substantial.

2. You are driving out costs from areas that customers do not use to make a "buy" decision (the "conventional operations" or "orthodox" parts of the organization).

3. You have compelling competitive advantages (the *strategy* of the organization) beyond price, and you *protect* those areas from the cost cutting.

You can't cut your way to success.

Cost cutting is a tactic (not a strategy) that should be applied to any element of the business that is considered table stakes in the industry. You should apply all the well-known techniques for efficiency to those areas of the business that are not true competitive advantages of the organization.

Other than that, remember that customers couldn't care less whether you are the low-cost leader. No customer buys from you because you need them to buy from you. No customer cares about whether you are earning a fair return on whatever you are selling; they simply evaluate the perceived value they are receiving for the amount of money they are spending.

There is a big difference between low cost and low price. In every industry and in every product or service offering, there is a group of customers that will only buy from you if you are the low-price leader. Chasing these customers is possible *only* if you are the low-cost leader.

Vanguard has long been famous for its low-cost approach to business. It pays lower salaries than its competitors, every investor is an owner in the organization (no third parties to pay), it eschews trying to beat the market (preference for index funds), it executes as few trades as possible, it has spartan offices, and it does not employ expensive "money managers." The result is an organization that consistently outperforms the other investment houses after fees are accounted for.

Anyone can be the low-price leader as long as they are willing to sacrifice margins. Competing to be the low-price alternative is a strategic spiral to mediocrity at best and bankruptcy at worst, unless you really are the low-cost leader at the same time.

So, low cost can indeed be a strategy—for *one* organization in each industry. It can be incredibly effective for that one organization, but it is only for one organization. Every other organization in an industry needs a real strategy (a set of true competitive advantages) that will be the focus of everyone in the organization.

The other part of this myth is the drive of an executive team to simply drive up revenue. In this pitch (which I hear over and over on earning calls), anything that grows the top line of the organization (sales in for-profit and donations/grants in nonprofit) is good. Besides the very obvious issue of "at what total cost" is this revenue being generated, this myth also ignores a fundamental part of the value equation for a strategist.

Think about Coca-Cola's splashy release of Orange Vanilla Coke in early 2019. The organization announced that it had taken their "innovation group" over a year to come up with this combination (a combination that every child can tell you about, having eaten hundreds of creamsicles in their life). They had an expensive Super Bowl rollout and had to clear shelf space, transportation, stocking, production SKUs, and the list goes on. All Coca-Cola executives wanted to discuss afterward was sales. We've seen the same thing with Tesla as they've lost hundreds of millions of dollars each quarter and only want to talk about sales.

As I mentioned in the introduction to this book, strategy is about achieving economic rents (returns) and/or social rents (returns). Those start as the net returns received by the organization that exceed the total variable costs of the new product or service. As each product or service is sold, it provides the organization with a real return. Over some period of time (if all goes well), those real returns add up to an amount that exceeds investment plus required rate of return. Achieving this is what strategy is designed to do.

There is only one low-cost competitor! Revenue is a necessity—strategy is about earning real returns.

Myth 7: Our Brand Is Our Strategy—We Call It Our Brand Strategy!

Brands are incredibly powerful symbols for both employees and customers. A well-crafted brand image consistently delivered upon can certainly draw in customers while allowing the organization to charge a premium price. However, a brand is *not* a strategy. It is the set of competitive advantages that underlies that brand that is the strategy.

Every organization has a brand, and we have seen brands come and go over the years. Sony was the pinnacle of technological innovation and a cachet in the 1980s, at a time when Apple was considered a niche player in the computer field. The names have not changed significantly (albeit Apple moved away from Apple Computer), and yet their "brands" are completely different. Sony was known as the technological leader in many areas of electronics, with a visionary understanding of what retail customers wanted. As competitors caught up, they failed to maintain that progressive edge.

Sears was the go-to store for decades. They catered to a growing United States and had the ability to deliver what you wanted wherever you were. As competitors grew their ability to deliver (especially to rural America), Sears fell further and further behind with no strategy being articulated that would draw customers back into the stores.

This ebb and flow of brands happens all the time.

Forbes produces a list of the most valuable brands each year, suggesting that indeed, brand value fluctuates. Take a look at the changes in the top five most valuable brands:[4]

2000	2010	2019
Coca-Cola	1) Coca-Cola	1) Apple
Microsoft	2) IBM	2) Google
IBM	3) Microsoft	3) Microsoft
Intel	4) Google	4) Amazon
Nokia	5) GE	5) Facebook

By 2019 only one of the brand names from the top of the chart in 2000 was still there.

---

4 https://www.interbrand.com/best-brands/best-global-brands/previous-years/2010/

It is important to understand that a brand has no value without a strong set of competitive advantages supporting it. As companies fail to continuously design and effectively implement real strategies, the brand loses value. Fortunately, for most brands, this decline is gradual, as customers have institutional memory. This provides a continuous window within which organization executives can develop real strategies that truly separate the organization from its competitors and then tie those elements to the brand name.

By itself, the brand name provides no reason for customers to buy. Great brand names have died over the years, not for a lack of investment in so-called brand imaging, but because the organization failed to deliver consistently on a strong set of competitive advantages: Pan-Am, Eastern, Blockbuster, Tower Records, Polaroid (and effectively Kodak), Circuit City, Napster, Texaco, Sharper Image, Woolworths, and the list goes on. At one point each of these companies was dominant in their industry. Customers went past their competitors to do business with them, and now they don't exist.

Brand is not a competitive advantage.

Myth 8: Say It Ain't So—Time for the Annual Strategic Plan

Somewhere along the way, strategic planning got inexorably linked to the concept of time. I guess this was inevitable. If tactical plans were short-term, then strategic must be long-term? Strategic plans were to be updated (or even completely revamped) on an annual basis. The key elements were to lay out three- to five-year goals and then set the organization forward toward achieving those goals. What quickly happened is that these annual rituals turned into budget forecasts and bonus bludgeons that had little to do with the reason customers buy from us.

Companies pour substantial effort into crafting a real strategy. That strategy is really made up of just two elements (as I discuss at length in this book). The first is bringing the table stakes (the "conventional operations" or "orthodox" expectations of customers and employees) of the business up to the median expectation of the customers. Most of what is done on most days at most organizations is simply the table stakes expectations of customers/employees. It is the blocking and tackling (sorry for the football metaphor) that is the very reason any customer considers buying from an organization. The second element is the effort to consistently deliver on several *true* competitive advantages such that your customers will go past your competitors and buy from you (preferably at a higher price, but just getting them to go past competitors and come to your organization is sufficient).

Strategy implementation is about driving these two elements as far and as long as we can. The more consistent you are with your employees and your customers, the more you will reap the rewards of a solid strategy.

When should you consider changing that strategy? There are four discontinuities that should trigger the executive team to reevaluate the strategy of the organization. Those four are changes (1) made by competitors, (2) instituted or proposed by regulators, (3) in the use of technology in your industry, and (4) socioenvironmental factors (recessions, oil price changes, inflation, etc.).

1. One or more of your competitors have closed the gap on one of your true competitive advantages such that the customer is struggling to see your advantage. We see this happen a lot! An organization is an industry leader in a particular area and simply cannot understand why customers won't continue to reward them for that initial leadership after the competitors catch up.

2. There has been a significant change in the regulatory environment that will impact on of your competitive advantages. Regulatory changes often affect an entire industry but can level the competitive field in a way that customers are no longer incentivized by your advantages.

3. There has been a significant technological change that impacts the cost, development and/or delivery of your product/service/offering. Technological changes can come from outside the industry, but it is when it impacts the expectations or behavior of customers that it must be addressed. For example, moves from outside the traditional watch industry (Apple Watch, iFit, etc.) caused a wave of change in consumer behavior. Demands by consumers to track products throughout their development have driven blockchain as an imperative in many industries.

4. Significant changes in the direction of society or activism can have profound impacts on the strategy of the firm. Nationalism moves can make formerly accepted practices obsolete, eco-activism can impact how products are produced and crops are grown, and the #MeToo movement brought hidden practices of organizations to light and caused substantial changes in their business practices.

A solid strategy approach is to constantly monitor these four aspects of the environment, looking for changes that could impact the organization's strategy. Typically we set up trigger metrics to decide when those changes have the potential to impact our business. At that point, the organization should examine the strategy and determine if it is still valid. If so, then keep the focus of all employees on the consistent delivery of the strategy. If these external impacts appear to have changed what constitutes a competitive advantage, then it is time to reexamine and recraft the strategy of the organization.

Strategy should remain in place as long as possible.

Chapter 2

A Strategy Model
That Works

Strategy is iterative, sequential, and continuous. There is a path to follow if you want to develop a solid strategy for your organization that separates it from its competitors. In this chapter I outline the approach and the fundamentals of the model. The chapters that follow will examine each element of this overall model in greater detail.

Depending upon the complexity of the organization, strategy design can be done at the individual product/service offering level, group or division level, or entire organization level. While it would be wonderful to have a singular set of competitive advantages that permeate the entire organization, the reality is that this is often not the case.

In order to determine where strategy design efforts should start, we have a rule of thumb that states that whenever there is a significant change in the comparison competitive set and/or a significant change in the perfect customer set, the organization will have to craft a unique set of competitive advantages. Quite often we find that some competitive advantages of the organization work with multiple parts of the organization. We might find that two of our competitive advantages align with every part of the organization, while each area has one or sometimes two additional competitive advantages unique to that area. I encourage organizations to try to find as much commonality as possible.

Strategy design starts with the organization as it exists *now*. You have sales now. The first questions that should be asked are what makes you unique *now*. After examining where the organization is now, we can move on to what the organization could do that would constitute a true competitive advantage.

Good strategy design starts outside the organization.

There is simply no way to develop a strategy without putting yourself in the shoes of the customer and viewing the choices for your product or service the way that customers see those choices.

Strategy starts with a deep understanding of the competition and at least a fundamental understanding of your current customers. Customers are constantly comparing your offerings with those of your competitors. From a strategy perspective, there are four key areas that need to be understood, all of which will be discussed in more detail in chapter 3.

First, every product or service offering has a perfect current customer. That is a customer who instantly gets the value proposition and is willing to pay you for it. The ability to articulate that in a way that all employees can recognize these customers is critical to success. These are the customers whom we want to listen to, take advice from, and work to retain while we determine what really constitutes our competitive advantages.

We will return to this perfect customer again after having crafted our real competitive advantages. A key element will be to use those advantages to determine precisely which customers would most benefit from our (now focused) value proposition and how to find those customers.

Second, a comparison competitive set must be established in order to evaluate your offerings relative to those of your direct competitors. Most sales are lost to a small group of "bump" competitors. That is, if you lose a sale, who did you lose it to? If you win a sale, who else did the customer consider? These are your bump competitors. Crafting a competitive set for analysis of your offering is a crucial step in not only attaining but maintaining a competitive advantage. You may lose sales to many organizations; however, research has found that customers (B2B or B2C) only evaluate three to five competitors when deciding where to make a purchase. With a little help from Voice of the Customer (VOC) research and some deftly developed analytics, this list can be established. We will discuss this along with median expectations and metrics.

Third, it is necessary to evaluate the offerings of your organization from the perspective of both real and perceived switching costs. Customers intuitively evaluate these two. A real switching cost is one that costs your customer real money or significant time to switch from you to your competitors (or vice versa). Perceived switching costs can be quite powerful as well, but they generally need constant reinforcement to be effective and cannot be proved.

Finally, it is important to map the touch points with the customer. Every touch point with the customer is an opportunity to press home the competitive advantages of the organization. The single biggest element in effective strategy implementation is the consistent delivery of the core competitive advantages. Mapping the touch points allows for the crafting of that message by the many employees in your organization who touch the customer.

01 External
Analysis

Once there is a solid understanding of the how the organization/product/service/ offering is viewed from an external perspective, we can turn our attention inside the organization. The first step in that process is to define the elements of the organization that are standard (ordinary, typical, orthodox, expected, table stakes, conventional operations, etc.) and which elements of the organization offering are potentially exceptional (extraordinary, remarkable, unorthodox, differentiating, etc.).

Half of strategy is ensuring that the organization is considered a player in the market. That is, the customer views the organization as having all the fundamental elements in place for the customer. Without this, the customer will simply rule out your organization from the consideration list long before purchase evaluation has started.

Most of what is done at most organizations most days are the standard, conventional (orthodox) operations that must be done by virtually every business in the industry.

We will discuss all this at length in chapter 4.

Standard Operations
What you must do to be competitive

Potentially Exceptional
Why people come the first time and return

		Do it
No	Standard	Do it well
Is this why you believe that people come the first time and return?		Don't be better than median
Yes	Potentially exceptional	Time to evaluate whether it is a **TRUE** competitive advantage

Knowing the elements of the organization that are standard allows us to establish those areas where resource investments can be restricted (as long as these are maintained at or near the median for the industry) in order to channel those resources into something that truly makes a difference with the customer. More importantly, an examination of these elements will reveal some (often many) that have fallen below median over time. These are those standard parts of the business that really frustrate your customers and employees. We will detail out the approach for determining these and developing project plans to bring them up to median.

Consider what you expect to see when you walk into an office building, restaurant, bank, or store. Much of what is done on a daily basis is the "blocking and tackling" that must be done for customer legitimacy. Lights, tables, merchandise, desks, phones, and ability to take payments are all stock expectations. Those expectations rise over time in virtually all industries (OK, not in the airline industry, which clearly has found that they can continually reduce the standard offering and still have a viable business). Median expectations of payment options, sophistication of web pages, access to information, and demand for transparency have all increased. These increases in median expectations by customers requires continual investment by the organization just to maintain a position where the customer will consider them when deciding on a purchase.

Those elements (resources or capabilities) that the business team believes have the potential to be separators—that is, potentially exceptional—can now be evaluated to see if they are truly competitive advantages for the organization. Each item that the team believes might be a real separator needs to be analyzed with some real science. Virtually all strategy academics and practitioners utilize some form of resource-based analysis (RBA) to determine what constitutes true competitive advantages. This approach was developed into a process in the mid-1980s and has become the predominant (and best researched) approach for determining competitive advantages.

RBA works well because four of the five elements are relatively orthogonal; that is, they lie in different quadrants and constitute unique looks at the same resource/capability that the business team thinks might be a separator. The fifth element of RBA considers an interesting area where corporate decisions can negate a resource/capability from being a real competitive advantage.

Back in the early 2000s, I along with a group of researchers modified the theoretical approach in order to make it more practical for business executives to use. A substantial history of research and practice suggested that most things fail at "rare," then "durable," and on down the list. Therefore, we recrafted the classic model to take this into account and save time in analysis. If you look up resource-based analysis (advantage) or its many, many variations (VRIO, VRIN, VRIST) you will find lots of examples and approaches. The approach used in this book is just one. It is one that I believe is the most practical.

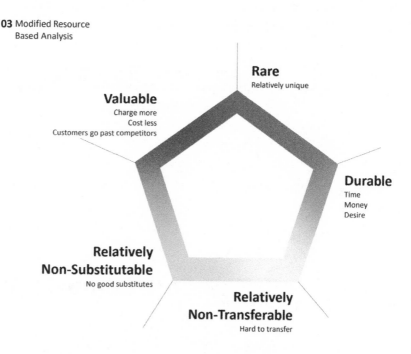

03 Modified Resource Based Analysis

We will discuss this approach in detail in chapters 5 and 6.

In order for a resource/capability to be a true competitive advantage, it must pass all five elements of the analysis. If it fails anywhere along the way, then we will not hang our strategy hat on that element. Please note that there is a *lot* of art in this approach. The science is to examine the same resource/capability through five different lenses (each of which has some very specific criteria), while the art is the team's assessment of those elements.

Once we have developed a short list of those elements that are true resource-based advantages—that is, those resources and capabilities that pass all five elements of RBA—we have the set of elements that constitute the organization's true competitive advantages at this point in the life of the business. The same approach will be used to evaluate all new potential competitive advantages in order to incorporate those into the growth model for the organization.

In order to be successful (profitable, growing), a business needs to have two or three true competitive advantages. If the organization has only one or even none (as happens sometimes), then the organization's leadership needs to craft together what they could do that would pass all five elements.

> *The future of the organization depends upon having two or three*
> *true competitive advantages.*

 **04** Sustainable
Competitive
Advantage

True Core Competencies

Those resources/capabilities that are **true** RBAs.

From this point forward in the analysis, the effort turns from strategy design to strategy implementation. Once the organization has a solid handle on what truly separates it from the competitors in the eyes of the customer as well what table-stakes elements need to be brought up to median, it is necessary to get the entire organization focused around those elements.

A great strategy must be communicated and rewarded through the entire organization in such a manner that every single employee in the organization knows precisely why the customer truly pays the organization. The goal is to get past feel-good pitches to customers and get to those elements that we can truly defend as the reasons for customers to choose our product/service/offering.

No matter what the marketing hype says, customers don't really buy a Rolex watch for its precision (they are not very precise; status is more important), a Cadillac

SUV hybrid for its fuel efficiency (there are far cheaper vehicles with better performance), Beats headsets for their low profile (seeing major athletes wear a set has a lot to do with sales), McDonald's salads for their health benefits (it's a compromise so that the kids can eat what they want to eat), or tickets on United Airlines in order to fly the friendly skies (in 2019, J.D. Power ranked United Airlines dead last in customer service among the five major carriers in the United States).[5] A focus on these types of elements of the business, while probably well intentioned (or perhaps it just feels safe), is a waste of resources on things that are at best standard and at worst well below the median expectations of standard.

Since it is the employees of the organization who deliver on the promises made, communication and transparency become critical for the success of any implementation. There are several areas to focus on in implementation: (1) the mission of the organization as it ties to the competitive advantages; (2) the vision of the organization, which should provide inspiration about where the organization wants to go; (3) the values/purpose, which are meant to guide the behavior of everyone; and finally, (4) the activity metrics that will be used to measure strategic success so that employees are clear as to what actions will be rewarded.

Although many organizations claim to have one or more mission/vision/values/purpose statements (or claim that there is no value in having any of these), the fact remains that these codified statements provide one of the most powerful, unifying communication tools for employees and customers alike. The mission statement in particular has tremendous immediate value if it is well written and tied tightly to the competitive advantages of the business. Having a clear, well-defined, codified, and real (actions are clearly emulated from the leadership team) set of values along with a purpose allows everyone in the organization to understand the common reason for why the organization exists and how it will do business. That, in combination with activity metrics (gates in some instances) tied to the strategy of the business, gives everyone a means of measuring actions. Strategy metrics are not traditional financial measures, customer counts, or satisfaction surveys. All established organizations have more than a sufficient number of these post hoc measures. From a strategy perspective, we need to be able to link activities with performance.

---

5 https://www.jdpower.com/business/
press-releases/2019-north-america-airline-satisfaction-study

Every leader has a set of hypotheses about what will work for their organization. They hypothesize that if we do X, then we will grow sales, increase profitability, etc. The question becomes, what activities need to be performed, and how will we know that they are being performed on a daily basis? The link between activities and performance is crucial if we are going to learn from our strategy efforts and be able to improve them over time.

Measuring and aligning activity to the strategy of the business is a key to success.

---

05 Mission & Strategy

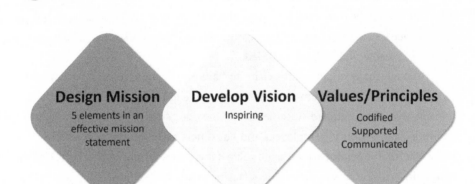

Design Mission
5 elements in an effective mission statement

Develop Vision
Inspiring

Values/Principles
Codified
Supported
Communicated

All of this must be communicated to the organization in a succinct, continuous, and consistent manner for everyone to get the message and apply it to their jobs. All of this will be examined at some length in chapters 7 and 8.

Structure Follows Strategy

The fundamental rule that structure follows strategy is lost in many organizations. The executives announce a new strategy and leave the structure as it was, or worse, they continually change the structure of the organization, causing upheaval among the employees. The next step is to use the structure of the organization to get the strategy implemented.

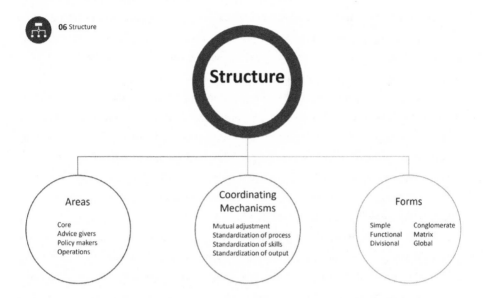

06 Structure

Unlike most books on the subject, which start with the type of structure (functional, divisional, etc.) and then use examples to try and align the strategy with the structure, I start with the strategy and work out to the type of structure. This well-developed approach was originally crafted by Henry Mintzberg in the late 1970s.[6] Research and practical application has modified this approach so that it can be utilized by any organization and ties the structure directly to the strategy. That process has three elements to it.

The first is to divide up the organization based on each area's impact on the competitive advantages of the business. Crafting together what groups should constitute the *core* of the business (the part most responsible for the competitive advantages) allows the organization to bypass so much of the internal squabbling about resource allocations and who makes those decisions.

---

6 Henry Mintzberg, *The Structuring of Organizations* (Englewood Cliffs, N.J.: Pearson, 1979).

The next two elements are the groups that constitute the advice givers and the policy makers. These are the groups within each organization that provide the knowledge "fire-power" to the core and the groups that protect the organization from legal, ethical, competitive, and regulatory problems. Policy-making groups have tremendous power in the organization to establish policies that must be followed by the core as well as the rest of the organization. Advice-giving groups do not set policy; instead they provide advice that can be accepted or rejected.

Consider the legal group within a typical organization. Some of what is done by this group sets policies that protect the organization, while other aspects of their work is to provide advice on various ways that the organization might operate. The two functions are quite different. In many organizations, anything that the legal group says is taken as *policy*, when much of it is subject to interpretation. Separating these people within the legal group provides tremendous clarity on which opinions need to simply be accepted and which can be interpreted.

Finally, there is the staff group. While this group is usually quite large and broken up into many parts within the organization, their primary responsibility is to run the table stakes parts of the organization. They need to do their job; they need to do it well. They just don't need to do it any better than the median expectation in the industry. These areas of the organization are the ones where the focus on efficiency initiatives and the processes that ensure consistency of performance are most critical.

Once these four groups have been determined, the next element of structuring the organization is to determine the best method of coordinating the work within each of those groups (and there will be many groups). How you coordinate the work of employees will determine how many managers you really need and the type of manager that works best. There are five significant coordinating approaches that should be considered, with three of them allowing you to have dozens or even hundreds of people reporting to a single person. Each area within each group should have the coordination approach fit their function.

The final element of structuring design is to combine everything above into a structure both efficient and easily understood. Far too much time is wasted by employees trying to figure out whom to work with in order to get something done. This complex and critical subject will be examined in chapter 9.

After structuring the organization, the final piece of the pie may be the most complex. It is the alignment of all the aforementioned elements. We generally break this up into four distinct efforts, with the last being the most powerful tool we have found in implementation.

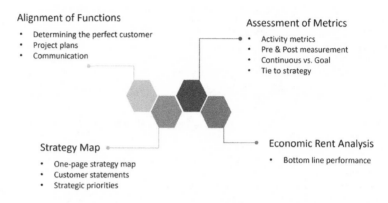

Alignment of Functions
- Determining the perfect customer
- Project plans
- Communication

Assessment of Metrics
- Activity metrics
- Pre & Post measurement
- Continuous vs. Goal
- Tie to strategy

Strategy Map
- One-page strategy map
- Customer statements
- Strategic priorities

Economic Rent Analysis
- Bottom line performance

This starts with reconsidering who the perfect customer would be for these focused advantages and how they can be identified. The aim of this process is to dramatically improve the success rate of sales efforts. We will aim to make this definition of the perfect customer very concrete and easily identifiable.

Then, each of the true competitive advantages along with the two "orthodox" elements (conventional operations) of the organization that the team has decided to tackle first must be developed into detailed project plans (why we choose only two orthodox elements will be explained later). Whether these are crafted as classic waterfall plans that cascade to completion with various sequential and concurrent elements or utilize some type of agile approach, they must be made as detailed as possible. Thinking through what must be done at the organization in order to drive behavior up front provides transparency (and timing) with the leadership team, the organization as a whole, and the board of directors. It takes most organizations an extensive amount of time before their actions translate into visible financial outcomes. During that time it is important for everyone involved to show that movement is being made. These plans need to incorporate the cultural issues that change will create.

A substantial effort must be made to translate the competitive advantages into metrics that can be benchmarked, tracked, and refined. As previously mentioned, strategy metrics are focused on the activities that deliver on our competitive advantage promise. We want to be able to go "eyeball-to-eyeball" with a customer and allow them to test us. If we make a strategic promise, we have to deliver on it consistently. The overall impact on the organization's financials are calculated, approved, and tracked. This leads to the development of the *strategy map*.

Every single employee in the organization (or group/product area, if need be) will have a single-page strategy map. That map is grounded in the competitive advantages of the business.

Strategy Map

Comparison Set:
Orthodox:

Unique Differentiators	Customer Experiences (Statements)	Strategic Priorities	Metrics
		What must WE do to Achieve (Project Plans)	

A critical performance element of strategy implementation is the ability of every employee to have an impact on the organization's strategies. This requires that they clearly understand what we seek to hear from customers about our competitive advantages (*not* the organization as a whole) and what the leadership expects in employee actions. The first column on the left consists of the concise representation of each of the true competitive advantages. The second column is where the organization converts the competitive advantages of the business into statements that they would want to hear customers make about the business relative to that particular competitive advantage. In the last column are the activity metrics that will be used by senior management and the board of directors to determine how well (and consistently) the competitive advantages are being delivered to the customers. The third column is there to remind everyone that the whole map is converted into project plans. Those project plans should involve everyone in the organization. This mapping technique, approach, and use will be discussed in chapter 12.

This model constitutes *strategy*!

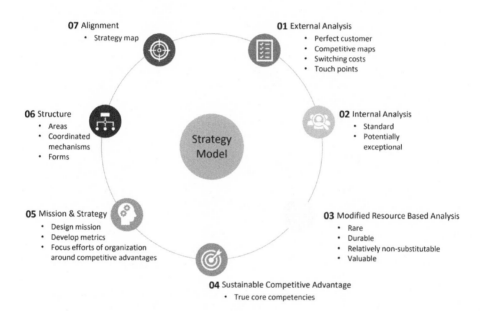

07 Alignment
- Strategy map

01 External Analysis
- Perfect customer
- Competitive maps
- Switching costs
- Touch points

06 Structure
- Areas
- Coordinated mechanisms
- Forms

Strategy Model

02 Internal Analysis
- Standard
- Potentially exceptional

05 Mission & Strategy
- Design mission
- Develop metrics
- Focus efforts of organization around competitive advantages

03 Modified Resource Based Analysis
- Rare
- Durable
- Relatively non-substitutable
- Valuable

04 Sustainable Competitive Advantage
- True core competencies

Chapter 3

Know Your Current Customers and Your Competitors

The path to a great strategy starts with looking outside the organization. There are many, many ways for organizations to dedicate enormous resources to understanding the market. Whole departments have been created to generate information and provide competitive intelligence. One look at any strategy textbook or a short conversation with one of the big consulting groups and you will realize that there are dozens of techniques available. My recommendations are relatively simple, extraordinarily easy to explain to employees, and provide sufficient insight into the competitive market for an organization to be in a position to craft a strategy. In this case, sufficient is not a bad word.

No amount of data analysis will provide you with insurance against bad judgment.

Generally, I prefer not to overkill the analysis. Use what you want or are comfortable with but ensure that you have a good grasp on your customers' perspectives of the market. Here are the six key approaches that executives should use to gain a strategic grasp on the competitive environment:

1. Develop a deep understanding of the current *perfect customer.*

2. Examine the industry and determine its current state.

3. Craft a comparison competitor list, narrow that list down to your "bump" competitors, and develop a deep understanding of how that group is winning their clients.

4. Classify the strategic approach used by each of your competitors (it will make a big difference in how they react to your competitive moves).

5. Examine the real and perceived switching costs from the customer's perspective.

6. Map all of the points where your business touches the customer, ensuring that every touch point reinforces the strategy of the business.

Current Perfect Customer

Every business that has sales has a perfect customer. A perfect customer, by definition, is one who

a. instantly understands your value proposition and

b. is willing to pay you for it.

I like to think of the perfect customer as the bullseye in the middle of a classic shooting target. At this point in our efforts, these customer groups are described somewhat generically for the industry. After we have crafted our *true* competitive advantages, this will be refined substantially for *our* particular organization (chapter 10).

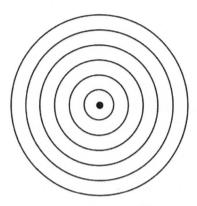

Consider who the perfect customer groups are for car rental agencies and their *gas option* (an over-the-top money maker):

1. the first-time renter who doesn't know the area

2. a business traveler (often on an expense account) who will be cutting it close to make the flight back out

3. international travelers (first visit to a country)

4. customers who rent the super expensive vehicles in the fleet

What could the rental car organization *really* charge these people? What could you offer that would compel them to bypass the competitors and buy from your organization? Another look at the rental car organization market is the one for unreserved vehicles late at night. Imagine it is midnight, and your flight has been cancelled. You need a rental car to get to your destination (only a two-hour drive away—something that has happened to me). What can the business charge? What is the compelling value proposition? Perfect customer! Or ponder the folks who used to stand in line at midnight to get the latest iPhone. What could you charge these perfect customers? They instantly get the value proposition and are willing to pay for it. The more compelling this value proposition is, the stronger your position to charge more.

Just consider how businesses develop. Every business that you have ever worked for, every business on the Fortune 500, and every business that you can think of started as an entrepreneurial venture that was created by one person or a small group of people. Over time, because they had a compelling value proposition and a set of customers that paid for that value proposition, they were able to grow the business.

At some point, virtually all businesses hit a wall with the number of perfect customers who are going to buy from them. In order for the organization to grow, the senior leadership team is forced to draw in customers who don't instantly get the value proposition and may not be as willing to pay the same price for it that the perfect customers are willing to pay. These new (nonperfect) customers must be incentivized to purchase (preferably without upsetting the perfect customers).

Senior leadership teams start making changes to incentivize and accommodate customers who are not perfect. Decisions are made that have the potential to not only impact the experience that the perfect customer has, but also destroy the organization's strategy, impact its net cash flow, and yet appear to be successful for a while because top-line sales go up in the short run.

If we could run a business that never had to move past the group that constitutes our perfect customers, we could constantly refine the offering and enjoy a business that perfectly matched our capabilities with the needs of our customers. Unfortunately, in order to grow, most businesses (OK...all businesses) must try to reach out and satisfy more and more customers. This is where companies develop problems. In order to attract these new (and significantly larger) customer groups, the organization resorts to a variety of strategy-destroying techniques such as

1. price reductions

2. sale pricing

3. discounting

4. special deals

5. cost savings measures that impact the customer experience

6. introducing more and more new products or services that distract from the original value proposition and cause logistical and procedural nightmares

7. outsourcing elements of the business that impact the customer experience

It is unfortunate for the long-term strategy that as the organization begins making these strategy-destroying moves, top-line sales increase or costs drop, and often, they do so quickly. Think about how Cross pens moved from being a special gift to being available at every drugstore.

Sales soared for a period of time as the image deteriorated, finally leaving the organization with higher overall revenue and substantially lower net income. Old US Airways (prior to the formation of American Airlines) outsourced elite traveler customer service to service providers in other countries. Their costs dropped dramatically in the short term until repeated complaints and defections to other carriers from their coveted business travelers finally forced a move back to North Carolina. The expenses incurred and the goodwill lost in this failed move impacted the organization for several years.

All companies seek to grow their market beyond their perfect customer base; unfortunately, there can come a point in all these moves where the organization goes too far and loses the perfect customer(s) that it once had. In some cases, this spells the demise of the organization. In other cases, the moves have been so slow that a new perfect customer group has been formed, and the business can thrive. General Electric has ebbed and flowed over the years such that today it looks nothing like it did in 1980. In the process, they isolated, packaged, and sold business units that had fallen from their famed number-one or number-two market share position. Many of those businesses were sold to organizations that thrived on that unit's particular perfect customer.

The key reason to develop a strong understanding of your current perfect customer is the guidance that it provides to management. We want strategic moves that are purposeful, consistent, long lasting, and considered. An understanding of the perceived perfect customer is core to the organization's ability to craft a set of competitive advantages. That perfect customer group will be refined and made explicit once we know the true competitive advantages of the organization. At this point the goal is to narrow the focus.

Obviously, we expect senior management to try and grow the organization. It is the focus on the perfect customer(s) that can provide the compass—but not a precise compass, as strategy is about nuance. I like to remind everyone that strategy is an "ish" approach. General direction will put your organization far ahead of your competitors.

How far can the senior leadership team push their organization past the perfect customer group, and can they pull it back when they go too far? Starbucks has been one of the greatest examples of this push and pull. Howard Schultz has proven his ability to master the focus on the perfect customer, flow the business out from that perfect customer, and pull it back when the business has strayed too far.

Starbucks's backstory is well-known, and the fact that Starbucks coffeehouses are ubiquitous is a testament to their understanding of the customer. The organization ventured from a classic coffeehouse (including selling mugs, etc.) to a seller of music, film, and books. The organization has experimented with beer service after 4:00 p.m. in some locations and bought out tea purveyor Teavana (an organization they failed to truly incorporate into Starbucks—they finally announced they would close down all Teavana stores by the end of 2018).[7] After rebranding the organization from Starbucks Coffee to Starbucks in early 2011, the organization has moved strongly into the grocery aisles, with a variety of products well beyond coffee (but it does include variations of Teavana teas!).

After stepping back from day-to-day management, Schultz returned to run the organization in 2008. The organization had faltered in almost every way possible. Howard Schultz wrote an open letter to the entire organization about commoditization and the need to return Starbucks to a unique position in the market. He noted that many of the decisions made during the previous few years had been well meaning and even data driven, but that the sum of the decisions resulted in the loss of the value proposition for the perfect customer. They had moved to automated machines that were so tall that you couldn't talk to the barista making your coffee. They produced vacuum-packed coffee with the unintended consequence that the customers couldn't enjoy the smell of ground coffee in the stores anymore. They used cookie-cutter store designs that felt institutional instead of the intended third place that Schultz had

---

7   Neil Stern, "Starbucks Forced to Continue Operating Teavana (For Now)," *Forbes*, December 6, 2017, https://www.forbes.com/sites/neilstern/2017/12/06/starbucks-forced-to-continue-operating-teavana-for-now/#6e40622c428a.

cultivated for decades. Starbucks had also started providing hot lunch sandwiches, which put smells into the air (think burned cheese) that had customers mentally comparing the business with fast-food restaurants.

He told the employees in his open letter (available on the web), "I have said for twenty years that our success is not an entitlement, and now it's proving to be a reality. Let's be smarter about how we are spending our time, money, and resources. Let's get back to the core. Push for innovation and do the things necessary to once again differentiate Starbucks from all others."[8]

Why does the perfect customer want to pay four dollars or more for a cup of coffee? Is it about being seen with the Starbucks cup? Is it about being able to craft such a complex order that no other coffee shop can provide the customer with exactly what they want? Is it about the baristas knowing customers' names and favorite drinks? Is it about having a unique language that makes you feel a part of a closed society (think Grande, venti, and trenta)? It is certainly something well beyond just the drink, and for the perfect customer, the value proposition is compelling enough to pay a *vast* premium for the cup.

This understanding of the current perfect customer group can be developed in many ways, but in an existing business, one of the best (and easiest) is to examine which customers consistently use your products or services and don't complain about the price! Ever watch people line up at an Apple store the day before a new product release? Wait in long lines to attend a movie? Put up with less-than-ideal conditions to buy something on Black Friday (or Thursday or Wednesday as the case may now be)? Wait in line for ten hours to ride the new Hagrid roller coaster at Universal Orlando? You get the picture. There are dozens (if not hundreds) of techniques that can be used.

Some of the most popular approaches are as follows:

1. **Most profitable customers.** When you are accounting for all the expenses that go into completing (and supporting) a sale, which customer groups account for the highest overall profit or highest profit margin?

---

8 "Text of Letter From Schultz To Employees of Starbucks," January 7, 2008, Wall Street Journal, https://www.wsj.com/articles/SB119974711738273245

2. **Repeat customers.** Which customer groups are regular, repeat customers *without* having to be incentivized by discounts or special offers?

3. **Brand ambassadors.** Which customer groups are the most visible proponents of your product/service/offering? These customers are often engaged with the organization on many levels. This includes being visible on many social media sites.

4. **Volume drivers.** Which customer groups can you count on for consistent volume sales that allow you to "keep the lights on"?

5. **Dependent customers.** Which customer groups are dependent upon your product/service/offering?

Use what works for you and your organization, but make sure you have put yourself in your customer's position. The crafting of this must be done in such a way that employees can readily identify the customer. Once you have identified the groups that the team believe are the current perfect customers, some effort should be put into verifying that the team was correct. This can be done with internal data analysis and some use of the voice of the customer.

Know who your current perfect customer is and be able to describe why you believe they are buying from your organization.

The Industry and Its Current State

Having a good understanding of where your industry currently is assists in the development of a strategy for the organization. Although a number of approaches could be used, one of the most straightforward is to look at it via a lens that was developed twenty plus years ago by a group of researchers.

There are fundamentally four types of industries: (1) straight line, (2) decision tree, (3) range, and (4) chaos. Once you can effectively classify which industry your organization resides in, you will be able to better classify each of your competitors and the types of responses they will have to your organization's competitive moves.

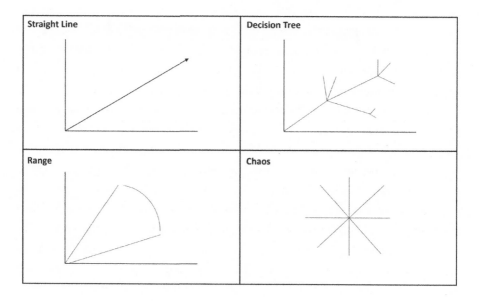

Type 1: Straight-Line Industries

As it sounds, this type of industry has very little variation over time. The railroad industry is an excellent example of this. The railroads around the world have set tracks to which they have access. There will always be a need to transport large amounts of heavy bulk items long distances, and therefore it is a safe bet that the railroads will be doing fundamentally the same thing in one hundred years that they do now (hopefully in a more efficient manner). The same approach can be used in many industries, from mining to museums to government operations to dry cleaners to mainline airlines.

Straight-line industries should demand continued investment in their core operations that are aimed at improving operations, reducing costs, and increasing knowledge. Competitors in these industries can expect that each will rigorously track and quickly follow any changes made by other competitors. Defensive positions are very strong, and virtually all innovative moves are quickly imitated.

Type 2: Decision Tree Industries

The majority of industries fall into this type and the next type (range). In this industry situation, there are a number of logical paths that companies can take, and once they take that path, it is extremely difficult to reverse course and chose another path. The beauty of knowing this is that those organizations that have taken a substantially different path from yours are highly unlikely to have much impact on your success and will for the most part not even respond to strategic moves that you make.

Consider even a very established industry, such as the automotive industry. While there are still "full-line" auto manufacturers, many organizations have chosen to go down a particular path that dramatically narrows their competition. There are ultra-high-end, truly bespoke companies that compete for a narrow market (e.g., Aston-Martin, Maserati, Rolls Royce, and Bugatti). Although they have periodically tried to increase sales to more mainstream customers, the reality is that they have gone down a path that would (along with investments in the business model) make it virtually impossible for them to compete with Porsche, BMW, and Mercedes-Benz. On another arm are the ultra-low-end vehicles (e.g., Tata, Chery, and Geely) that have made such great efforts to keep down the price of a vehicle that it would take decades for them to compete with Toyota, Ford, and GM. Even newer companies like Tesla have traveled down a path that is exclusively electric. It would be extraordinarily difficult for the organization to start offering internal combustion engines and would most likely destroy the organization in the process.

Most industries that have been around for a significant length of time have ended up in this type. The various players have chosen paths and narrowed their competitive market. Think fast food, clothing retailers, grocery stores, fast casual restaurants, coffee shops, banks, consulting companies, etc.

Type 3: Range Industries

Also representing the majority of industries are range industries. Range industries appear to have many, many possible paths for success. The differences between strategy approaches used by competitors can be very narrow. This is often the case, as an industry is really developing and what it might look like in a few years is unknown.

It is relatively obvious that current transportation network companies (Uber, Lyft, Ola, Waymo, DiDi, Cabify, and many others—more than one hundred at last count) are each pursuing a slightly different model for success. Just as with any industry, the table stakes expectations of customers have formed fairly quickly. Outside those expectations, the different models all appear to be slight variations of their competitors.

The result is a range of strategies with many, many competitors close by who could change quickly and match your offering.

These types of industries are more difficult to navigate and require a wider set of competitors for your comparison analysis. Industries that appear to be in this model include data analytics, AI, drones, cannabis, and blockchain.

Type 4: Chaos Industries

As the name suggests, this is an inherently unstable industry where the competitors have yet to figure out a viable business model, what the customer really wants, and where the industry will go even in the short run. This industry is typically seen at the outset of the industry development process and with industries that are solving wants for customers but just can't figure out how to do it profitably. The result is that competitors are all over the place with their strategies. Some are trying approaches diametrically opposite of others.

The electric scooter industry in 2019 seems to exemplify this. Many companies have poured into cities with their scooter offering. Some have docks, while most just let customers leave the scooter wherever they arrive. Some have sophisticated mechanisms for ensuring that riders follow the laws, while others just have a GPS tracker and payment system on them. Some companies are working with local government officials to become the exclusive scooter provider in that city, and others come in one night and unload hundreds (or even thousands, in one instance) of scooters randomly throughout a city and hope for use. There are variations in battery type, scooter type, and on-board offering. In addition, there is a lot of investment money being poured into the industry even though none of the competitors has made a profit. That said, the industry is projected to have revenues of over $51 billion by 2026.[9]

Comparison Competitive Set

Once you have a handle on your current perfect customer and the industry within which your organization operates, you can develop the comparison competitive set. It

---

9 https://www.marketwatch.com/press-release/
electric-scooter-market-size-to-reach-usd-51324-million-by-2026-2019-03-07

is important to understand that this is not every competitor that exists in your industry. Instead, it is that group of competitors that your perfect customer is using when they consider buying from your organization. We generally refer to this group as our "bump" competitors. Bump competitors are those competitors that you most often lose sales to and those who most often lose sales to you. If your perfect customer did not buy from you, whom did they buy from? If that perfect customer chose you, whom did they not choose in this particular instance? Why that customer bought is a whole different discussion.

In order to develop an effective strategy, it is necessary to have a comparison competitive set. Strategy is relative, not absolute. Your customers do not view the product or service offerings of your business in isolation from your competitors, and in that same vein, neither should you. The list of competitors must be actual companies, not generic groups of companies. Customers evaluate your product or service offering against other real companies, not concepts. In the best of circumstances, we strongly recommend that an organization (or a part of an organization, if the perfect customer changes from area to area in the organization) have no more than five competitors in the comparison set. Once the analysis gets above five, it becomes increasingly difficult to evaluate the strategy. Interestingly, most research suggests that customers narrow their comparisons down to just a few competitors when making a "buy" decision. This is true with both retail and commercial buy decisions.

Whom does Starbucks really compete with? It depends on which part of the business we are considering. Let's take the coffeehouse business and presume for a moment that their perfect customer stops by every morning on the way to work and orders a specialty drink (generally the same one every day)—you know the ones— iced, venti, decaf, thirteen-pump caramel, whole-milk latte. The only place that order would be understood is at Starbucks. The customer uses their loyalty app and could make the drink at home, but it takes time, lots of products, and a delicate machine. The customer prefers to grab a pastry (a decadent little treat that adds hundreds of calories to their day but is something the customer wouldn't even consider having in the house) with the drink. Look at the businesses that could be in their comparison competitive set (and I emphasize "could be," as I do not have access to their data):

1. **McDonald's**—Serves coffee and some specialty drinks, but it is hit-or-miss as to whether they will be able to make exactly what you want (they keep

tweaking their offering). They don't really have pastries, although they do have lots of food choices. They don't have a loyalty app at the time of this writing (amazingly), and the feel of the place is quite different. *Probably not a good candidate for the competitor list.*

2. **Panera**—They are able to handle the specialty drinks and have a good selection or pastries (probably a bigger one). They have a loyalty app and an easy feel that probably matches up well with Starbucks (usually a bigger area with more seating choices). *Good addition to the competitor list.*

3. **Dunkin'**—Generally offers basic coffee products (although they are also trying to expand their offering). No pastries, but a wide selection of donuts (equally decadent) and bagels. They have a loyalty app. The atmosphere is more austere and less welcoming to customers wanting to stay for a bit. *Probably not a good candidate for the competitor list.*

4. **Caribou**—Capable of making any type of specialty coffee or tea product that Starbucks can make. Equivalent pastry and food operation. Good atmosphere that competes well. Only open in eight states after the 2012 buyout by German organization Joh. A. Benckiser. *Probably still a good candidate for the competitor list.*

The list could go on to include some local coffeehouses or more international chains such as Tim Horton's or Caffè Ritazza that do a particularly good job, or you could include some of the companies that I ruled out. You can use data collected on customers to determine who else they consider when making a decision about where to buy (and doing so as confirmation after you have narrowed the field makes a lot sense). However, we have found that the leadership teams of most organizations do a very good job of narrowing this list. Despite what some might tell you, there is no scientific means for deciding precisely who should be on this list. Keep the focus on the perfect customer, use available data, draw inferences, be a student of your competitors, and establish your comparison competitive set.

Once this is complete, the organization needs to compare where they stand relative to that set of competitors. At this point in the analysis, I suggest that the organization use standard, easily collected metrics or metrics of particular interest to the organization at the time. Once the organization has figured out what their true competitive advantages are, they will be in a position to establish metrics more precisely aligned with the strategy. At this point, we are just trying to set a beginning point for discussion.

A series of two-dimensional charts can be used to graphically show relative position on each metric chosen. The vertical axis lists your organization and those in your comparison competitive set, while the horizontal axis represents the element being evaluated (whether it is quantitative or qualitative). Keep the vertical axis consistent, and the executives in the organization will have a set of charts that not only show where the organization exists in the present time but also can be used to track changes over time.

An example for a national B2C firm might look as follows:

Company X Competitors | Positioning Table

	Stock Products	Customized Products	Product Decoration (Screen Printing, Spray Frosting, etc.)	Product Innovation (i.e. SureHandle Technology)	National Mfg. Footprint (Short Lead Times)	International Mfg. Footprint (Short Lead Times)	Small Order Quantities Accepted	National Consistency in Offering	National Advertising Campaign	Specialty Contracts	Does Own Manufacturing	Sustainable Products Offered
Company X	✓	✓	✓	✓	✓	✗	✓	✓	✓	✓	✗	✓
Company Y1	✓	✓	✓	✓	✓	✓	✓	✓	✗	✓	✗	✓
Company Y2	✓	✓	✓	✓	✓	✗	?	✗	✗	✗	✗	✓
Company Y3	✓	✓	✓	✓	✗	✗	✓	✗	✗	✓	✗	✗
Company Y4	✓	✓	✗	✓	✗	✗	?	✗	✗	✗	✗	✗
Company Y5	✓	✓	✗	✓	✓	✗	?	✓	✗	✗	✓	✗
Company Y6	✓	✓	✓	✓	✓	✓	✓	✓	✓	✓	✓	✗

Each of these competitors should be researched by someone in the organization (or for the first time, you could hire an outside group to get the process started). Using the internet, available databases, industry association materials, publicly available stories, and industry experts (even former employees in your organization), the organization should be able to craft together how each competitor is positioned in the market.

At a minimum, the elements that should be examined include:

- firm fundamentals (industry, size, locations, etc.)

- business fundamentals (what they provide, to whom, processes, limitations)

- competitive advantages (what the organization pitches; what really separates them)

- areas of weakness

- financial capability (especially as it relates to their ability to respond to other competitive moves)

- recent moves (strategic changes, acquisitions, etc.)

Once developed, this should be maintained for each competitor so that the senior leadership team has a continuous picture of the competition as it moves and changes.

Classifying Competitors

Not all competitors are the same! Which of your competitors are (or should be) of most concern? Research in competitive analysis has found that the competitors that we should be most concerned about are those that have a desire (and of course the capability) to take our real competitive advantages (as well as those we craft in the future) and negate their value by turning them into ordinary expectations. That is, they either substantially match our competitive advantages before we can earn real returns, or they provide such a good substitute for them that it prevents us from earning real returns. Interestingly, not all competitors are really oriented in such a way that they can actually do this (despite what the media might suggest). Everything moves in an industry. The competitors make changes, the economy changes, regulations get changed, organizations lose key personnel, and there are social changes such that what were accepted business practices are no longer tolerated.

Raymond Miles and Charles Snow devised an approach to categorizing competitors that allows us to narrow the list of competitors to those most likely to challenge our strategy in the near term.[10] Every competitor can be divided into one of four categories based upon their propensities and way of operating: prospector, defender, analyzer, or reactor. While there is no hard line between these four categories, the general approach of each helps us decide which competitors are of most interest as we implement new strategies. Competitors move categories over time, especially when there is a significant leadership change, so it is still important to track their operations.

Prospectors. Prospectors are really defined by their inward focus. They tend to ignore or marginalize the efforts of their competitors. These types of firms are often seen as the innovators in an industry, as they are constantly releasing new products/services. This general tendency defies the state of the economy and is often a reflection of the leadership team. The nice thing about prospector organizations is that they don't respect the efforts of their competitors and don't react quickly to the moves made by competitors. This means that we (for the most part) take prospector organizations off of our list of competitors regardless of how influential they are in the industry. We can craft a set of competitive advantages and be fairly confident that the prospector firms will not make any immediate moves to take those away. In order to maintain a realistic focus on what might become industry standards, we typically add back in a single prospector firm to our comparison competitive list.

Classic prospector firms are always defined by time periods. No firm remains stationary. As mentioned previously, these organizations are most often a product of the leadership team. Some examples at various times in recent history (from my perspective) might include Southwest Airlines (airline—1980s and 1990s), Tesla (automotive—2010s), SpaceX (commercial space travel—2010s), Uber (transportation—2010s), Nucor (steel—1990s), McDonald's (fast food—1980s), Ford (automotive—1960s), Red Hat (software coding—2000s), Enron (energy trading—1990s), Sony (electronics—1970s), and the *New York Times* (news—2010s). Being a prospector firm is neither good nor bad, but when some of your competitors are prospector firms, you can

---

10 Raymond Miles and Charles Snow, *Organizational Strategy, Structure and Process* ([New York]: McGraw-Hill, 1978).

generally remove them from your list of competitors that you need to analyze and use for comparison.

Defenders. On the other end of the spectrum are defender organizations. These organizations are generally larger and are oriented around protecting their market position. A tremendous amount of resources is poured into cost containment, fast responses to challenges from competitors, discounting, and aggressive sales tactics. They are generally the second or third adopters of any new business approaches and are really only interested if it means that they can save significant costs. They are *heavy* users of the big consulting firms. They are willing to spend tens and even hundreds of millions of dollars to bring in "name" firms that promise them future cost reductions, efficiencies, or the ability to retake what they view as their market share. They also are very active in the acquisition market, as they try to "bolt on" firms that will shore up holes in their organization. They acquire to support and strengthen the orthodox elements of the business.

Much like prospector organizations, defenders are neither bad nor good. They can be very successful for a very long period of time. They are the main targets of corporate raiders because of their inability to grow substantially (they are oriented to protect) and the waste inherent in an organization that tightly controls all aspects (high bureaucracy).

Classic defender firms are also defined by time periods. Some examples at various times in recent history (from my perspective) might include Walmart (retail—2010s), Microsoft (technology—2000s to present), IBM (technology—1980s), Wells Fargo (banking—2010s), American Airlines (airline—for the past forty years), General Motors (automotive—hmmm...maybe the past sixty years?), American Electric (energy—forever), Sony (technology—1990s), and Caesars (gaming—2000s).

Defender firms should be in our list of competitors, as they are the most likely to aggressively attack any strategy efforts of our organization.

Analyzers. Analyzers are organizations that have the ability to effectively manage elements of both a prospector and a defender within the same organization. We say "elements" because these organizations are rarely (if ever) first with a new innovation. They carefully watch what other organizations release and observe consumer behavior before deciding to jump into the market. That market move is often done with a refined product/service offering that is resoundingly accepted by consumers. These organizations will often acquire more innovative firms in the hopes that one of their newer lines might provide a growth burst. In order to do this effectively, the organization must be structured to handle the two aspects separately (this rarely works under a single organizational structure—we will discuss this later in the book). As such, most analyzer organizations are relatively large with substantial resources capable of being deployed.

On the other hand, they have core elements in their business that they work to defend upon encroachment while investing in cost-cutting efforts. These parts of the organization are well known as the areas that provide capital to the rest of the operation. However, this organization is not nearly as aggressive about this defense (as it has newer elements being released regularly) and is willing to let market share slip in their established areas. They acquire firms that provide them with new growth areas.

Classic analyzer firms are also defined by time periods. Some examples at various times in recent history (from my perspective) might include Apple (technology—every time Steve Jobs was CEO and continuing under Tim Cook), Proctor & Gamble (household products—1980s and 1990s), Exxon (energy—2010s), Intel (technology1990s to present), InBev (beverage2000s to present), Facebook (media2010s).

Analyzer organizations should also be high on our list of competitors, as they carefully watch moves made by other organizations and seek to improve upon whatever is done. They have the resources and desire to compete.

Reactors. Reactors are an ineffective and ultimately destructive form of an organization. As the name suggests, they are very late to adopt new business practices or adjust to changes in the environment and appear to be rooted in what worked in the past as a guide to decisions. These types of firms are classic targets for bankruptcy and business raiders looking to break up the business to sell. The leadership changes often at these organizations, and yet they cannot ever seem to even catch up to the basics in the industry. Moving out of this propensity is extremely difficult once the spiral has taken hold in the organization.

Classic reactor firms are also defined by time periods. Some examples at various times in recent history (from my perspective) might include PG&E (energy—2010s), Sears (retail—1990s to present), Eastern Airlines (airline—1980s), Toys "R" Us (retail—2010s), Sports Authority (retail—2010s), Remington Outdoor (firearms—2010s), R. J. Reynolds (tobacco—1980s to present, in various forms).

Reactor firms are a bit of an issue. On the one hand, they are unlikely to really be able to take away any of our competitive advantages, as they struggle to simply function. However, they are wholly unpredictable in their actions and can pose a problem for our organizational efforts. We generally recommend keeping one reactor organization in the comparison list in order to address outlandish reactions that might take place.

This leaves us with a model for examining who should be in our comparison competitive set. We like to keep this set to something between three and six firms in order to be able to do a complete analysis and be able to model potential moves. Generally we would like to have

one prospector firm

two defender firms

two analyzer firms (or additional defender firms if there are not enough analyzer organizations)

one reactor firm

Crafting down the master list of all potential competitors using the techniques of industry type and competitor classification will allow the organization to focus on the most compelling competitors and their potential moves.

Real and Perceived Switching Costs

A big part of the value proposition is that every customer has their own set of switching costs when evaluating one competitor's offerings versus another competitor's offerings. There are real switching costs—those that require the customer to spend money in order to switch from your product or service to a competitor's or that require the investment of significant time (usually learning or setup) in order to switch. There are also perceived switching costs that, while relatively intangible, are nonetheless quite powerful. Perceived switching costs do not involve the expenditure of extra time or financial resources on the part of the customer, but they may be powerfully ingrained in the mind of the customer.

Real switching costs constitute a powerful set of real barriers for established organizations that can be tested. Once the customer of a bank has started a checking account, opened a savings account, established a safe-deposit box, and most importantly, taken the time to insert every one of their bills into the online bill pay system, the real costs for that customer to switch banks is significant. It is a time-consuming effort and therefore one that provides real switching costs.

The imbuing of real switching costs is a powerful barrier to new entrants and provides a means for organizations to charge more or ensure continued business (within reason). At some point, the bank could frustrate the customer (raise prices too high, treat the customer very poorly, fall behind in technology, etc.) to such a point that the customer is willing to incur the switching costs. By the same token, a competitor could expend the time, effort, or resources to reduce the switching costs to zero (or lower) in order to encourage switching.

Prior to the big recession that started in 2008, Bank of America (BofA) instituted an interesting program aimed at attacking real switching costs. They offered to pay new customers to open an account. Customers could open the account online and receive seventy-five dollars. The bet was that people would view the money as ample pay for the effort to open an account at BofA (reducing the real switching costs). Having paid the customer seventy-five dollars, BofA hoped that customers would discover for themselves how technologically adept the bank really was and move their account activity over to BofA. If you could accurately assess the amount of effort this would require and then calculate the value of your time, you could assess whether BofA had reduced your real switching costs to zero (or lower, in some cases).

Real switching costs come in many forms—loyalty cards for discounts (grocery stores), mileage programs (airlines), points programs (hotels), volume discounts (B2B), familiarity in function (cell phones), precise functionality (precision parts), and speed of payment (billing), to name a few.

Perceived switching costs are those costs that are far more intangible, but in many cases more powerful. These costs are those felt by the customer for the product, service, or organization. For instance, we could argue that there are no real switching costs associated with moving from Coke to Pepsi or vice versa. Both are quite easy to find and have virtually the same pricing, the bottles and cans open with the same ease, and you don't have to learn how to swallow all over again. Fundamentally, they both offer caramel-colored, sweetened, carbonated water. Yet, try to get a die-hard Coca-Cola drinker to switch to Pepsi. They simply cannot imagine holding the blue can or drinking it. Coke is tradition, while Pepsi is the new generation and hip. They have imbued these characteristics into the very essence of what it means to drink one or the other.

Consider what a Coca-Cola commercial at Christmas looks like. It is cute little polar bears sliding down a snowbank into a group of penguins and *not* eating the penguins. Amazingly, they all enjoy a Coke together. Can you just hear the following?

I'd like to teach the world to sing

In perfect harmony.

I'd like to buy the world a Coke

And keep it company.

OK, maybe not, but the essence is there. Pepsi is rock concerts, active people, and more importantly, the latest hip people. Over time, they have used Joanie Sommers, Michael Jackson, Ray Charles, Britney Spears, Christina Aguilera, and Beyoncé, to name but a few. Whoever is hot has a shot at being the next Pepsi idol.

These companies don't talk about the cleanliness of their commercial vats. They don't talk about the logistics systems, the bottling operations, the cool new features, and so on. Soda (and especially caramel-colored sugar water) has virtually no real switching costs. Just look at how many companies have tried to produce and sell the same stuff under their brand name (think Sam's Choice, RC Cola, Nehi, Double Cola, Jolt Cola, Schweppes Cola, or Like Cola, and you get the picture).

Perceived switching costs permeate the entire landscape of competitive choice. We have views about automobiles that generally have little to do with the data, as well as opinions about clothing, computers, restaurants, suppliers, shipping companies, and so on.

Perceived switching costs can be powerful, but they are also highly vulnerable. Since the customer can really switch quite easily, it is important to maintain the image rigorously and consistently throughout the entire organization. If we are the "fun ships" (Carnival), then we have to ensure that every employee understands what that means and is unflinching in its application. These perceived switching costs are glass houses for organizations, and they require extraordinary attention to detail by the leadership team.

It is ideal to have a nice mix of both real and perceived switching costs for the products/services of an organization. Carefully developed, they provide the backdrop for our pivot to examine the organization from the inside.

Touch Points

The final piece to the external examination (the foundation of good strategy) is the mapping of the touch points with the customer. Managing the touch points—those times when your organization has direct contact with the customer in any way—is an important part of understanding and later implementing the strategy.

A consistent element of strategy effectiveness has been the concept of *fit* and *alignment*. Customers judge an organization based on how much they can rely on a consistent experience. Any time that experience varies outside of a narrow boundary (for whatever reason), the clarity of the strategy gets confused for the customer. Unfortunately, confusing the strategy opens the door for the customer to consider other competitors.

Consider the way that you are treated at your favorite restaurant. Nine straight times you are approached for your drink choice within a minute of sitting down. The wait staff are attentive to your needs, and the food quality and portions are consistent. Then, on your tenth visit, everything is different. You wait much longer to be asked about drinks, you feel as though you are begging to get service, and the portion sizes of your meal are smaller. You make the decision to come again despite your misgivings, and the experience changes once again, with portion sizes back to normal but a long wait to be greeted.

The lack of consistency frustrates most customers and causes them to look around for alternatives. I've seen the exact same type of inconsistent experience muddy the compelling strategies in the relationships with manufacturing suppliers, law firms, lawn care professionals, hotel chains, internet providers, contractors of every type—you get the picture.

In order to really ensure, regardless of what is happening within the organization, that the customer has a consistent experience, it is necessary (or at least advisable) to map the touch points with the customer. Each customer interaction with any part of the organization should be tracked, scripted so that the experience is consistent, and aligned with the strategy goals of the organization. Do not miss a chance to bring home the reason that your organization has been chosen by the customer—hopefully one or more of your competitive advantages—with each and every interaction.

Mapping can easily be done pictorially, graphically, or in a spreadsheet (project-management-type tracking form) with the conditions as they currently exist:

1. every contact between an organization and its customers:

    a) all forms of advertising
    b) email/social media/direct mail
    c) websites

d) customer service/call centers

e) sales contacts

f) services contacts

g) product/service visuals

h) loyalty programs

i) news stories

j) volunteerism sponsored by the organization

2. the purpose of the contact from the customer's perspective

3. the strategy point(s) that the organization currently "messages" during the contact

4. the current result of the contact with the customer

It is an important baseline piece of information for the establishment of strategy, and once a solid strategy is in place, it is an important piece of the implementation of that strategy. After the strategy has been developed, the elements that need to be tracked will include the following:

1. every contact between an organization and its customers

2. the purpose of the contact from the customer's perspective

3. the strategy point(s) that the organization wants to "message" during the contact

4. the desired result of the contact with the customer

Chapter 4

Standard Stuff and Maybe Some Exceptional Stuff

Armed with a solid understanding of the market in which the business competes, we now turn our attention inward and examine the business.

Strategy consists of just *two* elements:

1. Half of strategy is maintaining conventional operations at or slightly above the median expectations of the customer. The only conventional operations elements that need to be evaluated are those that impact your ability to attain or retain customers *or* those that impact your ability to attain or retain franchise employees.

2. The other half of strategy is focusing the whole organization around two or three true competitive advantages so compelling that your customers will go past you competitors and come to you because of those advantages (without reverting to discounting).

One of the mistakes made by many, many managers, leaders, business owners, and executives (whatever title encourages you pay attention) is holding the view that everything in the organization has to excel. I had the following conversation with the CEO of a Fortune 200 organization.

CEO: "Look, Chuck, I've spent my entire life managing big corporations, and I view a business as a *boat*. I want everything in the organization to be the very best. I want the best manufacturing, the best sales force, the best payroll department, and the best administrative assistants in world. I push everyone to excel; I invest heavily in every area of the business so that as a whole we are the very best. It's like a boat. When you push everyone to the highest level and invest in every aspect of the business, then the whole boat rises."

Me: "Wow. It would probably be a useful analogy for the organization if it was a *boat*. But it is not a boat. It is an organization that customers buy services or products from, and no customer has ever come in the front door and said, 'Well, I just want you to know that I've heard you have a first-class payroll department, and because of that, I bypassed all your competitors to buy from you.' Customers could care less about your payroll department, your new agile approach to IT transformation, the quality of the cash registers, the health care benefits you offer employees, how much money you spent on the chairs in the executive reception area, or the new procedures you have for handling customer calls. These items are standard. That is, they are the things you do and have to have in order to be considered a viable alternative by a customer. Standard elements of the business are not why customers choose one business over another, but they are the important table stakes to be in the game."

Virtually every organization (OK, every organization) can be separated into those areas that are standard and those areas that are potentially exceptional (we'll get to that in a minute). Most of what is done, most days, by most employees constitutes the standard operations of the business.

- The standard operations of any organization must be done. If you fail to meet the standard expectations (for your business) of your customers, then they will stop buying from your organization.

- The standard operations of any business must be done well.

- However, the standard operations of any business need only be done at the median expectation level relative to the comparison competitive set.

What constitutes these standard expectations is decided upon by the customer as the customer compares our operations to that of our competitors. Furthermore, the level of expectation is always moving up. What was once special, unique, rare, or even a competitive advantage becomes standard over time. Customers' expectations are constantly moving up.

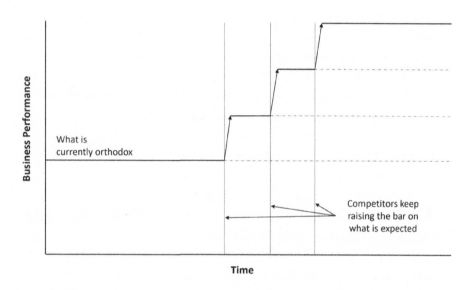

Organizations that started up their web pages in the 1990s were cutting edge. Today, we not only expect to find everything on the web; we also expect to transact much of our business that way. A cell phone in the 1990s was able to make a phone call (some of the time). Today, we barely care if we can make phone calls. Most of the wireless companies have moved to unlimited calls, because the name of the game is data. Not that long ago, college applications were tedious affairs involving a lot of paper and overnight delivery. Today, the whole process is done electronically, much to the dismay of FedEx, UPS, and other carriers. The list goes on and on, with obvious ramifications.

Meeting the median expectations for the conventional elements of the business is crucial to the success of the business. Imagine being at a high-end restaurant and having dirty silverware at your table. You send it back, and what comes back is more dirty silverware with old food encrusted on it! We have an expectation that the silverware will be clean. We don't really know what clean is (the presumption is that if we don't see anything on it, then it must be clean), but we want to believe it is clean. Businesses must meet the median expectation of the customer to be considered.

The restaurant could buy a $1,500 power dishwasher for the kitchen and meet the median requirement of most customers. If the organization bought a $30,000 high-end *super* dishwasher, the customer would not know the difference and would not care. Appearing clean is appearing clean. The organization simply spent all the extra money on something that was standard.

Imagine the same high-end restaurant. You go to the restroom and enter a neglected toilet area—a hanging bulb, broken mirrors, doors without latches, and the distinct smell of...! While this type of restroom would be accepted as median at a low-rent pub, it is unacceptable in a high-end restaurant. We have median expectations that are relative to the competitive set. You could overspend on the restroom as well. Customers will not pay you more money for a restroom that costs twice that of your competitor, nor show up more often because of the elegant sinks. Exceeding the median expectation for standard elements of the business is simply wasted money.

This is one of the *keys* to repurposing money and managerial time in an organization. Anything that is conventional operations needs to be done, and done well, but no better than the median expectation of customers. Remember that half of strategy is achieving and maintaining the conventional operations of the organization at or near the median expectation of the customer. Once you determine those elements that are below median and impact your ability to attain or retain a customer (or franchise employees), a key strategy focus of the organization must be organized to get those elements to median.

02 Internal
Analysis

Standard Operations
What you must do to be competitive

Potentially Exceptional
Why people come the first time and return

		Do it
No	Standard	Do it well
Is this why you believe that people come the first time and return?		Don't be better than median
Yes	Potentially exceptional	Time to evaluate whether it is a **TRUE** competitive advantage

The processes to accomplish this are relatively straightforward. Every activity of the business must be examined relative to the comparison competitive set. The employees of an organization usually have a pretty sizable list of areas where they believe the organization is failing to meet the expectations of customers. This is a good place to start and typically provides more than enough areas to address.

Each of the items that employees believe are below the median expectations of customers' needs to be examined relative to the competitive set. We then categorize those into three buckets: (1) areas that must be addressed because it is clear we are behind the industry in them, (2) areas where we are clearly at or near the median expectation relative to competitors even though we believed that we were not, and (3) areas that we simply cannot determine at this point.

Since there are usually more than a few areas that make the "we are definitely behind the industry" list, research into strategy implementation suggests that the leadership should take two of those items and focus the organization's efforts on bringing those up to the median in the industry. We do this with classic project plans (discussed later in this book). We know what the metrics should be because these are simply standard expectations in the industry. We should know how to get this done as well, as these are the standard operations of our industry.

> *You will get a better bang for your dollar by cleaning up orthodox areas of the operation than you will from all the competitive advantages you can craft.*

A world-renowned chef will be negated by dirty silverware or a subpar restroom. What quality of pen needs to be at the table in a bank? Apparently, not very good ones. A bank that decides to put out Mont Blanc pens for customers to use will not only lose a lot of pens (no chain will hold back those customers), but also will have spent a lot of money on something that customers consider standard. By the same token, constantly having pens with no ink or not providing pens might cause customers to look elsewhere and not even pay attention to the high rates that bank is offering.

The goal is to clean up as many of these orthodox areas of the business as fast as possible. By focusing the efforts of employees on just two elements at a time, you achieve quicker results and encourage employees to engage. It is tempting to try and attack all the orthodox activities that are below median, but that is a recipe for disaster. A year later, you will be back in the boardroom talking about the exact same problems. Focus and completion are a key part of this aspect of strategy implementation.

The steps in this process are:

1. Have employees recommend their top three areas where they believe the organization is substantially behind competitors in standard operations *and* where that impacts the organization's ability to attain/retain customers or franchise employees.

2. Investigate where competitors are relative to the list generated above and categorize each recommendation into one of three categories:

   a) must be addressed

   b) don't know if we are below median

   c) not below median and does not need to be addressed at this time

3. Using any of a dozen approaches (easiest to address, most impact on customers, cheapest to address, most complex to address, etc.), the leadership team should pick two areas to address first.

4. Project teams and project plans with hard deadlines should be formed to bring these areas up to the median in the industry.

5. Since these activities are the standard operations of the organization, metrics and processes should be well known.

The second half of strategy design is to determine what might constitute a set of compelling competitive advantages. A long history of research findings and practical experience with organizations would suggest that most organizations have at least one true competitive advantage even if the whole organization is not focused on it. In order to be successful in the longer term, it is necessary for every organization to have two or three true competitive advantages. Those must either currently exist within the organization or be developed in the near term.

Consider why you believe customers buy from your organization. Ultimately, we are looking for the few resources or capabilities that encourage your customers to bypass your competitors and preferably pay you more money. These are the elements that will constitute your competitive advantage.

This generally starts internally with a master list of everything that anyone in the organization believes *might* be a competitive advantage. Ask your employees:

Why do you believe that customers buy from your organization?

What makes you special in the market?

What are the areas where customers chose to pay us more than they pay competitors?

Armed with this list, we will be able to use a modified version of resource-based analysis to examine each resource or capability that the team believes might be a competitive advantage in order to figure out which of those are *truly* competitive advantages.

Moving this list from potentially exceptional to truly exceptional is the focus of the next chapter.

Chapter 5

A Modified Version of Resource-Based Analysis

R esource-based analysis (RBA) and its many variations, called VRIN, VRIO, VRIST, or half a dozen less-popular names has been the predominant method for determining true competitive advantages since the early 1990s. Some version of the approach has been around since the 1930s, but it was the move from the theoretical to the practical that really changed the fortunes of so many companies.

This approach was modified over time to make it more easily applicable to businesses. In multiple strategy textbooks and articles, I further modified the approach to take into account the realities of busy business executives. The theoretical model has been flipped on its head, as our consulting work repeatedly showed that there was no need to do the grinding work of determining how to attain value from an advantage unless that particular resource or capability had already passed through the other four elements. In the theoretical model, this value determination is done first.

There are five elements that must be examined for each resource or capability that your organization believes might actually constitute an advantage in the market. These elements examine the same resource/capability from different perspectives, providing a holistic look that imbues some real rigor. Each resource/capability must be

1. rare,

2. durable,

3. relatively nonsubstitutable,

4. relatively nontradable, and

5. valuable.

A resource or capability has to pass all five elements for it to constitute a true competitive advantage.

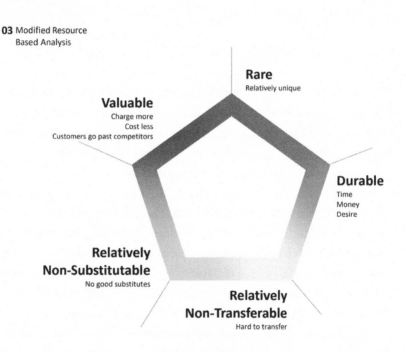

03 Modified Resource Based Analysis

Rare

What makes a resource or capability rare? It requires an honest evaluation of whether the team believes that it is really unique when compared to the comparison competitive set. The rule of thumb in the application is that if one other competitor is doing *to no more than our offering... providing same* [handwritten marginal note, partially legible]

the exact same thing as your organization (and even doing it just as well), we still consider it rare. If more than one is doing so, then we fail it at this step.

Resources and capabilities have to be unique (or relatively so) for our organization to have an opportunity to enjoy extraordinary returns. Customers will not reward you with extraordinary returns for simply doing the standard, expected elements of a business.

The evaluation of whether a particular resource or capability is rare should be done both quantitatively and qualitatively. Practical, real data on what a competitor is doing goes a long way toward answering this question. The resource or capability advantage we claim must be so clear that we can defend it with customers. Some elements of the customer evaluation will be unquantifiable (some real and some perceived). The management team needs to discuss these in their evaluation of whether some element is rare. The science is the honest evaluation of the resource or capability relative to the competitive set; the art of this effort is in the determination of the leadership team.

By definition, if something fails at being rare, then it is standard (orthodox), and we know what to do with it (do it, and do it well, but you don't need to do it any better than the median expectation of the customer).

Fails—It is standard.

Passes—Move on to evaluate durability.

Durable

Evaluating whether you believe that a resource or capability is relatively unique compared to your competitors is not only a crucial first step; it is also the step where most things fail. If it passes, then we need to examine whether it is durable. That is, will we be able to hold on to this rare resource or capability for long enough to earn extraordinary returns? A new idea or an existing resource or capability is only of value if the organization can capitalize on it to improve the economic situation of the business. The longer our organization is able to maintain this as a relatively unique resource/capability, the longer we have the potential to earn those returns.

Goal *exceed IRR*

Every industry is different, and that means that what constitutes the necessary time frame will vary. In the online women's clothing industry, the time frame for something to be considered durable is quite short, while in the offshore oil gasket industry, the time frames are very long.

You are trying to estimate how long you might be able to capitalize on this unique resource or capability (which passed the rareness test earlier). We tend to display this on a two-dimensional chart, much like a project projection chart.

The horizontal axis is time, and the vertical access is money. If we have something that we believe is rare at the current time, then it is incumbent upon the management team to estimate how long they will be able to hold on to that uniqueness. Just like so much of management decision-making, this is really a hypothesis that should be crafted by a knowledgeable management team.

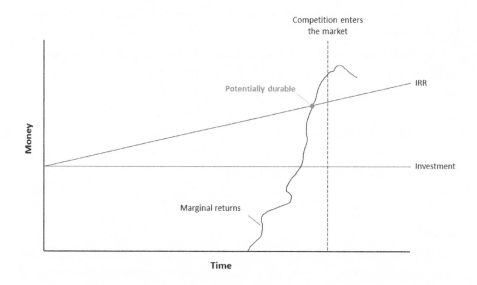

If we are trying to create a new competitive advantage or to focus the organization around an advantage that we believe we already have, then we can estimate the amount of money that we will be investing going forward (although companies are notorious for not accounting effectively for people's time in these estimates). That baseline is then modified by the required rate of return for the organization (hurdle rate, weighted average cost of capital, IRR, or whatever the organization likes to call it). For a competitive advantage to provide the organization with real economic returns, we need to be able to exceed that line before one of our competitors enters the market.

Strategists care about returns—not just top-line sales. You should estimate how long it will take from the decision to invest to the point where the organization will achieve its first sales. Then estimate the potential *marginal returns* for each sale—that is, the net returns received by the organization that are over and above the total variable costs of the new product or service.

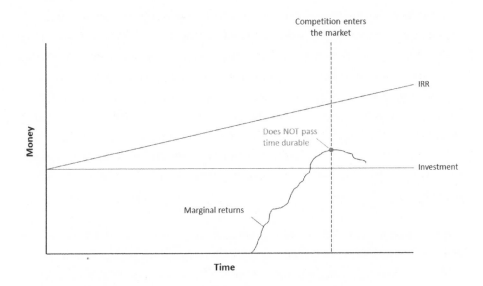

If we estimate that one of our competitors will enter the market prior to our marginal returns exceeding the required rate of return line, then what we are considering is not durable from a time perspective. While returns certainly don't plummet, they do start plateauing and then drop as new entrants capture value. There are many products and services that might exceed their investment, but only the ones that exceed the organization's required rate of return have the potential to be true competitive advantages and contribute to the success of the organization.

Durability has three aspects to it:

1. organizational capability

2. financial resources available

3. strategic desire

While they are relatively distinct, there is some crossover in concept. It is far more important to evaluate each potential resource/capability that passes rare through each of these three lenses than it is to be precise as to which delay category something falls into.

All three should be viewed from the perspective of the competitors trying to capture your customers, and while all three fundamentally translate into a time lag, each should be considered separately. Passing any one of these elements means that the resource or capability you are examining is durable. That is, if any one aspect of durability will cause a sufficient delay in competitive matching, then the resource/ capability passes durability. If it is durable, we move on in the analysis. If it fails at all three of these elements, then it is not durable and is no longer a potential competitive advantage. Each competitor must be examined individually. However, each competitor only needs to fail on *one* of the three elements of durability to allow us to move forward with RBA.

Organizational capability. Every organization has its own unique ability to make changes in response to competitor moves. Each competitor has organizational capability issues that might delay or improve their ability to respond. With RBA, we are most interested in organizational capability issues that would ultimately distract and delay a competitor from responding to our strategy. Elements of this that delay your competitors' ability to respond might include: (1) recent changes in the senior leadership team, (2) product recalls, (3) bad press for actions taken or not taken by the organization, (4) capacity issues, (5) high employee turnover, (6) administrative approaches higher in bureaucratic control and risk prevention, (7) HR practices that limit new learning, (8) recent merger and acquisition activity at the competitor, (9) recent cost containment moves, and (10) major deficiencies in their own standard operations.

Financial resources available. If the management team determines that they will be able to hold on to the rare resource or capability for a period of time that allows for returns that exceed the required rate of return because a competitor does not have the organizational capability to match them before we can earn real returns, then we must consider whether the competitors have the resources to match or exceed the resource or capability.

This is simply an estimate of whether you believe the competitor has the ability to make the investment (and again, each one must be evaluated separately). Due to poor business conditions, poor management investments in the past, weak growth in sales, lots of capital already committed for other projects, or investment in a different market segment, the organization may not be in a position to make the required investment to match you in the short run. While this look at your competitors logically bleeds over into organizational capability (how fast they can even move) and desire (whether they even think you are right), we try to separate the look in order to thoroughly open our eyes to the competitive threat.

Strategic desire. The last of the three aspects of durability is the interest of the competitors in trying to match your competitive moves. Are the competitors even interested in pursuing the RBA that you have (or are considering)? As we have seen, some competitors are (or should be) watching for any significant changes in competitors' business strategy. The best thing that can happen for your organization is for the competitor to think you are doing something that they would not even consider. That lack of desire to follow you translates into more time to enjoy the fruits of the competitive advantage.

Sprint moved aggressively to offer customers the chance to upgrade their phones twice a year when their primary competitors (Verizon and AT&T) had established the principle of phone replacement every other year. The bet by Sprint was that those companies had no desire to compete with Sprint in this area, as they were benefiting financially with maintaining two-year contracts. After fuming about the decision and complaining about the Sprint moves, they partially followed by allowing consumers to trade in more quickly (at a substantial cost). That lack of desire created a time lag that may translate into a sufficient window for an organization to achieve extraordinary returns. In this case, the competitors had the resources to invest in this approach, and it would not take long to change their systems to accommodate. However, they had no strategic desire to do so. This would pass the durable test.

Another aspect of strategic desire is to examine the strategy focus of your competitors. Where do they believe they have true competitive advantages? Where are they investing resources? What do they say about their focus/investments on analyst calls and press releases? The leadership team needs to evaluate whether they believe each of the competitors has the strategic interest in addressing moves made by your organization.

Examine each competitor for each of the three elements of durability. Once you believe that a competitor will be delayed by one of the aspects, you can set that competitor aside and examine the others. What we are hoping to find is that each competitor will be delayed by one of the three aspects (more than one aspect is just icing on the cake) such that we believe we will be able to benefit from the competitive advantage beyond the point of earning real returns.

What do you do with something rare but not durable? This depends on whether the resource or capability is one that you have now (where the goal will be to focus the organization around that resource/capability) or something that you are considering developing as a true competitive advantage. If it something that you have now (and yet it fails durability), you may continue to do it until your competitors actually match you. This should not be one of the core elements of your strategy, and you should not tie up too much of the future of the organization on something that your competitors can easily match, but rather enjoy what you have while you have it. If this is something that you are considering doing because no one in the industry is doing it right now (it is exciting and new)—*don't do it*! These types of creative, innovative ideas happen all the time. They are only of strategic value if you can hold on to the uniqueness long enough to earn real returns. Why increase your expenses, do all the hard work explaining the new product / service to customers, and raise the expectations bar if you cannot hold that bar for a period of time that will result in extraordinary returns? You don't. Put it in a file somewhere and wait for your competitor to do it.

Uber created a whole new industry by utilizing known technology and applying it to a shared economy model. Each new move by Uber is rapidly matched by their competitors around the world, with Uber taking the business hit from development. This includes efforts to get rideshare services legalized in various cities and countries, enhancements to their app model, changes to driver compensation, and alternative uses of the platform (e.g., food delivery). They have not developed a single true competitive advantage. While the organization has grown quite large, it has yet to even get close to turning a profit. Coming up with two or three real competitive advantages will be the key to long-term success.

Sun Tzu's *The Art of War* tells us that a key to success is the elimination of the competitors' advantages by the simplest means possible, so that our competitive advantages can win the day. At some point, one of your competitors will do a SWOT analysis and come up with an idea that is not durable (remember, they are just as smart as you and are thinking about all the same things...we just hope that they are not as sophisticated in their strategy approach). When they do, they will tout it as next best thing in the industry. You will know that this thing they are pitching has no durability, so dust off your files and bring it out. You will make whatever your competitor just did standard in the industry.

Relatively Nonsubstitutable

If the potential competitive advantage has passed as rare and durable, you are through the most important elements of the analysis. Most resources and capabilities fail at these two stages. Whereas the first two elements of RBA specifically address your competitors, the next two elements examine many peripheral areas that can impact the success of your efforts. These next two areas are easier to consider, and their evaluation is significantly more subjective (as if the first two were not sufficiently subjective for you!). The next two elements (nonsubstitutable and nontradable) examine companies not in our comparison competitive set. We have already examined the direct competitors with rare and durable.

There is a substitute (usually many) for every resource or capability that any organization has or will ever have. If there were truly no substitutes, you and your direct competitors would have 100 percent of the market. A substitute can be offered by every competitor that you did not put on your comparison competitive list. In order to get down to four to six direct competitors, you may have eliminated most of the prospector and reactor organizations. You most likely eliminated smaller or regional organizations. Substitute organizations are simply other ways that a customer attempts to attain a similar "value proposition."

The key to this element is to put yourself in the chair of your customer and consider the alternatives. The unique aspect of this look is to consider alternatives offered by those companies *not* in your comparison competitive set. You have already examined the competitors (rare and durable); now the effort turns outside the direct competitors. How else can the customer attain some similar value to the resource or capability you are considering? The second part of this examination is whether you believe that these are good substitutes or not. There is no further science to this. You can do customer studies to gain some insight, but at the end of the day, the management team needs to decide that they believe the substitute is either good or not good.

If there is a very good substitute available in the market, then this is not a competitive advantage. Once again, if you are currently doing it, you should continue to do so. If you are considering it, you should probably stop considering it and move on to other resources or capabilities—I say "probably" because this call is quite subjective.

Take a look at how this might work. The business world is all abuzz about social networking. An organization takes a look at their comparison competitive set and decides to engage in a full-on social networking blitz. They set up Instagram, Twitter, Facebook, and LinkedIn accounts, create customer and supplier blogs, start a series of podcasts, start video-sharing, run a rating service, and develop comprehensive data mashups. The effort is substantial and focused. None of their comparison competitive set is doing much more than the most basic types of social networking—and the leadership team passes it as rare. As they analyze each of their competitors, they find that each has the organizational capability to add this into their business models. The investment needed is moderate, but let's assume that each of the competitors has the financial resources to do this. As the leadership team looks at the strategic efforts of their competitors and they find that none of the competitors appear to have any interest in pursuing this approach. Therefore the leadership team passes this as durable.

What about nonsubstitutable? There are many very effective substitutes for communicating with customers, suppliers, and employees—email, letters, brochures, phone calls, sales visits, advertisements, and so on. Do you believe that these substitutes—many of which have been around as long as businesses have been businesses—are good substitutes for the new social networking blitz contemplated by the organization? If they are, then this fails at nonsubstitutability, and you move on to another potential resource or capability. If the management team believes that these are not effective substitutes, then you move on to the next element in the model and examine it for tradability.

Relatively Nontradable

If the resource or capability has been determined by the management team to be rare, durable, and relatively nonsubstitutable, then it is incumbent upon the team to determine if it is relatively nontradable. Tradability has to do with how easy it would be for your competitors to obtain the resource or capability from *you* and whether it is something that you even have the ability to trade.

This may sound a bit strange at first. Why would you sell something that the team has already determined to be rare, durable, and relatively nonsubstitutable? Companies do it all the time, often for very logical reasons. If your organization can sell some aspect of the organization and *not* tear the organization apart in the process, then it may provide cash to refocus the organization or change the direction of the organization. This is why many companies set up independent and autonomous business units. Doing so provides the overall organization the ability to sell off that unit without destroying the organization. Doing so also virtually guarantees that the business unit and its resources/capabilities are *not* real competitive advantages.

I usually put this whole element into perspective. Remember that the resource or capability that you are considering has already passed as durable. Therefore, you have ruled out most of the obvious considerations of whether the resource or capability can be obtained in the open market (a product, a consulting service, or a piece of equipment, for instance). The part that you have not considered is whether your organization can easily trade whatever it is to a competitor without losing the essence of the organization.

Here are several potential answers to the question you should ask about whether a particular resource or capability is tradable:

Is it tradable?	"Not without losing the essence of our organization!" Then move on in your analysis. This *passes*. You will not sell it. (Coca-Cola is not about to allow other companies to use their Coke formula.)
Is it tradable?	"We hold the patent on the Intellectual Property (IP), product, etc." It depends on whether you believe that the patent is tied to the essence of your organization. If it is, then move on. This *passes*.

You control it and won't let it go. If it is not, then you can choose to sell it or not. (Clear Collar held the patent on transparent cervical collars. Selling the patent would have shut down the business.)

Is it tradable?

"We have an exclusive license for X amount of time." Then move on in your analysis. This *passes*. You control it and most likely can't sell it! (An exclusive license to sell a product in North America for the next ten years cannot generally be sold to another organization. It is not yours to sell.)

Is it tradable?

"We don't own the concept!" This is the tricky one. If you have passed it thus far (and this is the big question with this particular aspect), *and* you can't control others using it, then this *passes*. (Offering breakfast items all day long at a fast-food chain is a concept that the fast-food chain does not own or control and one that probably would have failed much earlier in RBA. Starbucks uses many Italian terms for its products but cannot stop anyone else from using these; however, speaking "Starbuckian" may have made it to this point in the analysis.)

Is it tradable?

"We bought it from another vendor, and it is not exclusive!" Then you are done. This *fails*. You can't control its distribution to your competitors. You probably should have failed it in durability already! (We have the fastest car wash conveyor in our area. Unfortunately, we bought it from a vendor that would gladly sell it to any of our competitors.)

Is it tradable?

"We have the particular resource or capability set up as a unique business entity." Then you are done. This *fails*. You can trade it away. It is not that it is good or bad; it is simply that you don't want to hang your strategy hat on something that the next CEO can simply sell. (Our R&D operation is set up as an independent entity. It is easy to sell as a unit.)

Tradable analysis is really just a clean-up stage in RBA analysis. Whereas the other four elements (rare, durable, relatively nonsubstitutable, and valuable) populate separate quadrants of the evaluation approach (that is, they look at unique aspects of the same resource/capability), relatively nontradable is more of a threshold criterion in the analysis. Analysis of this aspect has generally found that it only eliminates a very small percentage of resources/capabilities that have passed up to that point. However, it is a critical threshold analysis to complete.

Valuable

Having used this approach with hundreds of organizations, I find it interesting that the theoretical resource-based approach (and the one often pushed by some consulting companies) starts with the analysis of value. As I mentioned at the beginning of this chapter, the approach is variously referred to as VRIO, VRIN, or VRIST, as well as a dozen or more names made up by various consultants and pop-management "thought leaders" (a term that I find particularly humorous). Each variation has elements of the full RBA approach that are organized a bit differently. The order matters if you value your leadership team's time.

More than two decades ago, I also used the classic approach. The organization executives would grind through the process of determining the value for every resource and capability that they thought might be exceptional, only to have one after another fail at rareness. My experience with RBA has been that most things fail at rare, the next most at durability, next at nonsubstitutability, and finally at nontradability. I can see no reason for executives to spend their time evaluating whether a particular resource or capability is valuable unless it actually can get to the value evaluation.

Virtually no other area in strategic management has been studied in more detail than value creation. It basically boils down to three key means of attaining value. Because you have something rare, durable, relatively nonsubstitutable, and relatively nontradable, you have the ability to charge more than your competitors, have a lower cost basis than your competitors, or get customers to pass your competitors and buy from you because you have this element. In order to pass the value test, you only need one of these three to pass (although to get more than one is fantastic).

Charge more. I am a fan of charging more when we have a real competitive advantage. If you have something simultaneously rare, durable, relatively nonsubstitutable, and relatively nontradable, then why would you not charge more for it? Over and over, I'm told, "We can't charge more because we are in a dog-eat-dog business. If we raise our prices, we will lose sales." If what you have has truly passed the previous elements (that is, you can go eyeball-to-eyeball with a customer and prove that you have a real advantage that is well supported), then charging more should be a practical and realistic goal.

Lower the cost basis. If you can't charge more (there are many reasons this might be the case), then maybe it provides value because it will lower your costs relative to your competitors'. Your organization would get the benefit of a better basis-point run by having a lower-cost structure even if you charge the same amount as your competitors. This can come about for a variety of reasons, including administrative culture (ability to make decisions faster), historical artifact (your facilities are located in lower-cost environments), process issues (the organization investments in process efforts have led to a more efficient operation), and a knowledge-based approach (your organization has been able to develop an approach that incorporates experience-based learning). Whatever the reason, the ability to have a resource or capability at a lower cost will provide competitive value for the organization.

Draw the customer past competitors. The final means of attaining value is the ability to draw customers past your competitors. That is, having a particular resource or capability encourages customers to bypass your competitors and do business with your organization because you have this particular resource/capability. It is the ability to draw in customers that you have not had before along with getting current customers to bypass competitors that propels your organization's growth.

The trifecta is to be able to do all three. Charge more, have it cost you less, and have customers go past competitors. However, if it passes for any one of these three value elements, then it passes our modified version of RBA.

We always start this analysis with current resources and capabilities. Those that pass all five elements constitute the foundation of the sustainable competitive advantages for the organization. Then the organization should move to evaluate potential resources and capabilities with the same model. All organizations should be continuously looking for new competitive advantages. RBA provides a means of evaluating which of those might provide the organization with substantial success.

The goal is to have two or three *real* competitive advantages upon which the organization can anchor its strategy.

Chapter 6

Sustainable Competitive Advantages

Once the organization has determined the resources and capabilities that they currently have as an organization, it is imperative that the organization use the same approach to craft and assess new ideas for the business. All this must be completed before we talk about how to implant this in the organization.

Think about the many companies that have seemingly evaluated new, bold moves only to have them fail to create value for the organization. Even though something might pass RBA, it is not a guarantee of success; it is simply an effort to add some significant science and a process that enables the leadership team to sort through many competing priorities.

JCPenney

When Ron Johnson was hired away from Apple to run JCPenney, it was assumed that he would bring some creative, unique thinking to an old-line retailer that had been stuck for a long time. He did that, but in the process, he allowed his creative flair to take him well beyond what could plausibly be considered competitive advantages in the eyes of his perfect customers. The execution of the plan eliminated the reasons that current shoppers were buying before new shoppers could be attracted. Let's take a look at a couple of his ideas to understand how he and the leadership at the time were able to pass these through RBA.

Assume that the comparison competitive set for JCPenney was Macy's, Target, Kohl's, and maybe Sears back then (if we are generous). Also assume that the perfect customer was a mom looking for bargain but also quality clothes for her family. Remember that how you set these elements dictates much of the strategy work done afterward.

Potential RBA 1

Elimination of house brands in favor of name brands from Martha Stewart and Joe Fresh. [11]

Rare? Yes. All the competitors had a mix of house brands alongside name brands. In a detailed RBA analysis, we would examine each of the competitors here and analyze their mix percentages. I've shortened this analysis for readability.

Durable? Yes. It appears that the other competitors all had the financial capacity to pursue this same approach with the exception of Sears (depending upon how you view their loss).[12]

	Revenue	Operating Income (Loss)
Macy's	$26 Billion	$2.4 Billion
Target	$69 Billion	$5.3 Billion
Kohl's	$19 Billion	$2.1 Billion
Sears	$41 Billion	($1.5) Billion

Since I believe that Sears did not have the capability to match this move by JCPenney, Sears would not be in a position to match the effort before JCPenney could have achieved real returns. Therefore we do not need to evaluate Sears any further in the durable analysis. We will continue the analysis with the other three competitors.

---

11 Note that we use RBA to represent the tool resource-based analysis as well as the individual perceived and actual competitive advantages with resource-based analysis.

12 https://www.macrotrends.net/, https://searsholdings.com/press-releases/pr/275

Organizational capability is a wide ranging and often qualitative analysis. While it would take some time to eliminate the house brands and institute this on an organization-wide basis by Macy's, Target, and Kohl's, it is doable within a reasonable time frame. The caveat might be the exclusivity of the contracts. Macy's, Target, and Kohl's were set up with a divisional structure with sales/profit goals. They each certainly had the internal skill set to transfer from a mixed portfolio of brands to all outside if they wished to do so. As such, all three of the remaining competitors have both the financial resources and the organizational capability to match JCPenney quickly if they wished to do so.

It is with strategic desire that JCPenney felt each of the competitors would not quickly match the move being made. Macy's had been on a multi-year effort to increase the number of house brands within the organization. They offered dozens of these throughout their operation while also selling several third-party name brands. Their strategy direction did not suggest a desire to eliminate the house brands. Therefore Macy's passes as durable. Target had significant house brands in clothing and groceries that had been a core part of the business for decades. Their profit margins on those were substantially higher than third-party name-brand goods, and they had invested heavily in the category growth. Target passes as durable. Kohl's has been developing their house brands for many years. They were known for their mix of name-brand goods along with very affordable house brands. The organization strategy was aimed at more control over brands, so it is unlikely that they would abandon all store brands. Therefore, Kohl's passes as durable.

Remember that we only need one of the three aspects of durable to pass for each competitor for that resource/capability to be classified as durable.

Relatively nonsubstitutable? No. There are many effective substitutes for this. There are stores that specialize in name-brand merchandise at reasonable prices that are not in our comparison competitive set (Dillard's, Belk, Stein Mart, Marshalls, and even TJ Maxx, among others). This *fails* at this point, and we would *stop* the analysis. However, for argument's sake (and obviously for the leadership at JCPenney at the time), let's suggest that you disagree with me and believe that these substitutes are not good ones. You pass it and move on. The key here is to evaluate where else the customer could achieve relatively the same value proposition and whether you think it is equivalent.

Relatively nontradable? Yes. This approach is a concept. JCPenney does not own the concept. Therefore, it is relatively nontradable. They don't own it to trade it! This passes.

Valuable? Could JCPenney charge more? Yes or no, depending upon your perspective. The name brands certainly could be sold for more, but this ignores the significant drop in sales that might occur with the higher priced clothes. Will it cost less? No. These contracts will have higher costs than the house brands. Do they have the ability to draw customers away from competitors because they offer this? Maybe. The plan was to draw in customers who were looking for name brand goods. So, if the organization could attain the aforementioned exclusive contracts, then they might draw in new customers, but perhaps at the cost of some of their current customers.

Conclusion: I would have failed it at nonsubstitutability. However, a case can be made to pass it all the way through (which Ron Johnson, the board of directors, and the senior leadership team obviously did).

Potential RBA 2
Scrapping the pricing policy of marking up prices and offering discounts with lots of promotions and coupons. Prices would be set lower (accounting for what JCPenney really earned after all the discounts).

Rare? Yes. None of the competitors were doing this. All four of the competitors had a long history of coupons, sales, and bargain racks that they viewed as core to their business model. Again, each competitor would be analyzed here to discuss the number of sales and coupons offered per year or per season to show how what JCPenney planned to do would be rare. For brevity I have eliminated that analysis from here.

Durable? Yes. I pointed out the financial capability of each competitor previously. Sears was not in a position to respond financially, while the others most likely were. Therefore we continue the analysis with the other three.

Organizational capability does not change either. Each of the three remaining organizations is organized to address this potential advantage.

Strategic desire only varies in the amount of dependence each has on discounting/sales. Kohl's entire business model is based upon discounting goods; therefore, it is highly unlikely they would want to move to a model of simple pricing. Target and Macy's heavily rely on sales events to draw customers into store. Macy's gears a big push on sales from well before Black Friday through Christmas that is tied to the Macy's Thanksgiving Day Parade. Target uses sales racks to draw customers around the store in a hunt for bargains. Each seemed unlikely to abandon that practice, and therefore this approach appeared to be quite durable.

Relatively nonsubstitutable? No. The substitutes include online retailers such as Amazon offering set prices without advertising or coupons and companies like Walmart that offer "low prices every day." Another substitute would potentially be flash-sale sites or simply companies that continue to offer coupons. In my estimation, this *fails* at this point, and we would stop the analysis. However, again let's suggest that you disagree with me and believe that these substitutes are not good ones (again, clearly what was done by Ron Johnson and the leadership team at the time). You pass it and move on.

Relatively nontradable? Yes. It is a concept that JCPenney does not own and cannot control. They would not be able to prevent anyone else from doing it, and since they don't own it, they cannot sell it. Therefore, it is relatively nontradable.

Valuable? Could JCPenney charge more? No. They dramatically lowered prices, but they hoped to achieve the same true returns. Will it cost less? Maybe. They were hoping for significant savings by eliminating the coupons as well as eliminating the staff that ran more than nine hundred promotions a year while eliminating the staff to change items in the stores. Will it draw in customers? Maybe. The plan was to draw in customers who were tired of having to search for bargains and wanted a fair or consistent price—similar to the CarMax approach.

Conclusion: I would have failed it at nonsubstitutability. However, remember that this is a hypothesis—the analysis that is done is both art and science. A case can be made to pass it all the way through (which Ron Johnson obviously did).

I may not have mentioned this before, but you have to love strategy (or hate it, if you need guaranteed answers). There is *no* "right" answer. This is all interpretation. What I would like to add to the mix is a well-tested approach that requires management to evaluate a decision from many angles prior to implementation. However, as I stated early on in this book, there is a lot of art to strategy. When a decision has to be made, science can only take you so far; you must make a decision.

Bird Scooters

Let's take a look at another recent example. Bird is one of the dock less electric scooter companies that are all the rage. Bird has launched their dock less scooters in cities all over the United States and is expanding into other countries. Like most of the scooter companies, you download the app and pay one dollar to start riding, and then there is a per minute charge for use. They can be picked up and dropped off virtually anywhere, often causing a cluttered mess on sidewalks. As of mid-2019, Bird received over $700 million in funding and was valued at just over $2 billion.

Most of the companies have simply moved into a city and started operation without any permission or licenses. They typically hire local contractors to pick up the scooters at night, recharge them, and place them back on the streets by early morning.

Let's presume that their competitors as of 2019 are Lime, Spin, Jump, and Skip. Let's also presume that the perfect customer for Bird is an urban professional who cannot easily use public transportation to get to the exact location they wish to go. They are looking for a faster way to cover short distances within a city where the trip is too far to walk comfortably (especially in the heat) and too short to use a car service (taxi, Uber, Lyft, etc.). Remember that how you set these elements dictates much of the strategy work done afterward.

Potential RBA 1

Scheduled delivery to your home.

Rare? Yes. Each of the four competitors require you to go to their scooter, whereas Bird will deliver a scooter to your doorstep by 8 a.m. Lime has a GPS locator via mobile app. However, customers must go to the scooter. Jump also utilizes a GPS locator via

THE STRATEGY MINDSET 2.0

its app. The Jump app uses Uber so that customers can call an Uber to take them to the nearest scooter. Spin also offers an app with a map for customers that shows where the scooters are, and the same holds for Skip. Since none of the competitors had this capability, it passes rare.

Durable? Remember that there are three aspects to durability, and we are looking for at least one that will delay any response from one of the competitors.

Financial capacity. Lime received $467 million in funding and had a valuation of just over $1 billion. Therefore, they had the financial resources to respond quickly. Jump received $100 million in a partnership with Uber, providing them adequate resources to compete. Skip had raised only $31 million, making it very unlikely that they could compete financially. Spin raised just $125 million; however, it was via a blockchain offering, and it was not obvious that they could raise more money.

Based on this, I would say that Spin and Skip do not have the financial capability to respond. This means we only need to examine Lime and Jump for organizational capability and strategic desire.

Organizational capacity. Lime has established a methodology whereby scooters are dropped off in group locations around the city. They have not established the infrastructure to handle this; however, it does not seem to be overly complex, and it appears they have an equivalent organizational approach. Jump is really an almost wholly owned operation of Uber. Uber clearly has the organizational ability to deliver vehicles to precise points, and one would assume that Jump would have access to this as well. Therefore, both of the remaining competitors have the organizational ability to quickly match Bird.

Strategic desire. Lime appears to be in a growth mode for the near future. They are trying to quickly grow the number of cities in which they operate. They don't appear to have an interest in adding this complex and relatively smaller option at this time. Jump, being a part of Uber, is absolutely not interested in this option. One of the pitches made by Jump is that you can call an Uber to take you to the nearest available scooter. The business model appears to be one oriented to increasing Uber rides as well.

Based on the logic above, it appears that this potential advantage passes durable.

Relatively nonsubstitutable? Yes. One substitute might be using a bike share. While it's a relatively equivalent form of transportation, one would still have to find a bike pod or a bike near their location. At that time this book was published no bike share companies delivered a bike to your house. Also, a bike is a bigger, more difficult piece of equipment. Whereas many (illegally) ride their scooters on sidewalks, virtually all bikes must be ridden on the street, which exposes the rider to more vehicles. A second substitute might be purchasing your own scooter. It is relatively expensive to purchase a motorized scooter ($1 thousand or more), the customer is responsible for charging it, and it must be protected against theft. Neither of these look like good substitutes.

Relatively nontradable? Yes. It is a concept that Bird does not own. They cannot sell the idea and cannot prevent anyone from doing this. Therefore, it passes.

Valuable? Could Bird charge more? Yes. This is a valuable feature, and one would believe customers would pay extra for this convenience. Would it cost less? No. This would be a more expensive approach for the organization, as they drop off one scooter at a location rather than a group of scooters. Would it draw in customers? Yes. There are customers who would view this feature as a reason to stay with Bird and to use Bird over the other companies. This particular advantage had two out of the three means of attaining value be positive.

Reality is that once we have determined that something could be a *real* competitive advantage, we would make the effort to do some research to determine if we had all the facts correct and do some pricing/demand analysis before we moved forward. However, this approach allows us to narrow down what should be researched to just those elements we believe have the potential to provide us with sustainable positive economic returns.

The crafting of a set of true competitive advantages is critical to the success of any organization. These are the true differentiators! This is *strategy*!

Chapter 7

Have a Reason for Existence—Mission/Vision/Values/Principles

Let's be honest. I believe that it is relatively fun to work through what constitutes your organization's competitive advantages. It takes some discipline and effort on the part of the team to put aside preconceived notions of competitive advantage, along with a willingness to think creatively about where the organization has true advantages. However, it is the fun part of strategy. It is much easier to figure out what you should do than it is to actually do it. Far more people plan out an exercise regimen than actually follow through with the effort!

Implementation of strategy is the focus of the rest of this book. It is difficult and frustrating to implement a strategy, but without it there is inconsistency, mediocrity, or worse.

Getting all or even most of the individuals in an organization to move in generally the same direction is infinitely more difficult than the old EDS commercial that extolled the virtues of herding ten thousand cats across the open plains! I firmly believe that the majority of the employees at any organization go to work every day with the intention of working hard, doing something of real value for their organization, and finding a personal or professional sense of accomplishment. The real question that should be asked is, "Does the team running the organization have any idea what they want their employees to actually do?" I believe that the resounding answer with many organizations is *no*!

Why is your organization in business? While it is probably to make money (or assist those in need, for nonprofits), this most certainly is not the reason that customers purchase anything from the organization. Customers will never purchase a product or service because the organization needs to make money (unless you are very good at begging).

Imagine this mission statement: "As our fiduciary responsibility is to maximize shareholder value, we strive to make the most money possible within the legal restraints of the countries within which we do business."

Interestingly, everyone in the organization would understand that their job was to pursue any type of profitable business activity that was legal. The employees would explain to customers, suppliers, and fellow employees that the organization is trying to make as much money as possible, which is why they are charging more, requiring concessions, demanding reduced prices for raw materials, etc. It is not their fault; they are simply following the mission. Furthermore, everything in the known universe would be on the table for consideration. The organization would have the flexibility to morph into anything it desired, regardless of its current direction or capability. Employees (much like cats) would be all over the place, pursuing whatever they thought was going to make the most money.

If you have done a good job developing your competitive advantages, as discussed in the previous chapters, then those advantages should be the cornerstone of why customers buy your product or service.

The reason that companies are in business is to provide a needed or desired product or service to a group of consumers in such a manner that those customers are willing to profitably compensate the organization in exchange for that product or service.

Once you have developed your true competitive advantages, it is the job of the senior leadership team to get everyone in the organization to consistently move in somewhat the same direction.

Since strategy can only be implemented by the employees of the organization, employee participation and embracing of the strategy efforts has the biggest impact on the success of the organization. There are three core elements of strategy implementation that tie everything discussed in the rest of this book together: (1) communication, (2) willingness to serve, and (3) common purpose.

The leadership team must communicate the strategy (competitive advantages and orthodox fixes) to all employees in as many methods as they can. Employees will respond to organizations where the communication is clear, honest, repeated, and rewarded.

To start that communications effort, there are several overarching elements of the organization that must be addressed:

1. the mission

2. the vision

3. the values/principles (its moral compass)

Mission

The first step in the implementation effort is designing the mission statement for the organization. The mission is directly tied to competitive advantages of the organization and is about what we are trying to accomplish right now. It is both a part of the communication effort as well one of the ties to a common purpose for all employees.

A mission statement has a unique ability to focus the efforts of every employee in the organization if, and only if, it is designed well and is implemented with a singular focus that places it above all the daily firefights at the organization. Every employee trying to "do good" in the typical employee's day is insufficient for the firm to truly set itself apart from the rest of its competitors. What one employee believes is "good" may exactly counter another employee's interpretation of "good." On even a small scale, this creates a situation where everyone is working extremely hard, and yet the firm seems to constantly achieve only average returns, customers are confused about the "message" of the organization, and the ability to grow the business is hampered.

The goal of strategy is to achieve extraordinary returns within the organization's industry. I have been examining mission statements for the past two decades and have concluded that they tend to fall into one of five categories. Take a look at the various types of missions provided to employees at many organizations today, and you quickly realize why the cats are running all over the place.

Remember: It is not that the cats are doing anything inherently wrong; they are just being cats, and they will not get to any "end" as a group unless they are given a goal, a reason, and a reward.

Mission Statement Type	Implied Goal	Employee Reaction
1. The well-designed mission statement	Senior management knows where they are taking the organization and works with employees to keep it topmost in their minds.	Empowerment! Employees have a tangible direction.
2. The "we finally have a mission statement—now get back to work" statement	This mission thing is not very important. Just make money. We put this out for the public and the analysts. It is full of words that no one can really disagree with!	Embarrassment! Ask these employees about their mission, and 20 percent can tell you what it is (sort of), but they quickly admit that is not what they do each day and doesn't really matter.
3. We have no mission—would you consider a "vision," "statement of purpose," or "overarching goal"?	Specificity is just not our thing. We'd prefer to be vague in the short term.	We loosely know what we want to do right now! Good thing that this statement doesn't affect me day to day.
4. We're not sure who we are, but we have "values."	As long as our employees honor these values, we can do anything.	Confusion! Corporate assets are continually spent in an attempt to define the value concepts, while the organization spends inordinate efforts to examine all possibilities for growth.
5. Statements might restrict our options, so we have none	We'll do anything to make money, increase market share, or grow the organization.	Desperation! Organization resources are poured into any possibility for growth.

The Importance of Direction

An organization of people exists to accomplish what the individual cannot accomplish alone. The most pressing issue that develops as the organization grows is one of coordination. As Henry Mintzberg pointed out many years ago in his definitive book on structuring organizations, the issue of coordination is the continual struggle to get employee effort focused on the unique mission of the organization.

Once you have figured out what constitutes the competitive advantages for the organization, the implementation of that strategy (the competitive advantages) logically begins with a useful, focused mission grounded in those advantages that every individual in the organization can use to make decisions. Well-trained, motivated employees lacking an effective, unifying mission will head in the direction that they—individually or in small groups—believe is the best for the organization. This may or may not align with the focus of the top management team.

Despite all the interesting books calling for the top management of companies to be inclusive, bottom-up, consensus-building, congenial stewards of organizations, a simple fact has remained a constant: it is the responsibility of senior management to set the direction of the organization and to ensure that everyone works in unison toward that effort. Take the responsibility to accomplish this task.

My father was a navy ship commander in the Second World War. Once he received his orders, the entire crew was put to the task of attaining success in the mission. He depended on each crew member being an expert in their particular task, and yet he also depended on all of them working together to accomplish the mission that he laid before them. Imagine, if you will, the typical corporate scenario at play aboard this naval war ship. We don't know exactly where we're going, but we want to be very efficient. We hire good people and tell them to "do good." People in each area of the ship concern themselves with improving their operations and arguing in meetings that their needs are supreme. Each area of the ship receives award after award for their outstanding performance, but the ship wanders the seas.

In a long history of looking at mission statements, researchers and practitioners have almost universally acknowledged the value of a singular mission as a driving force for companies and yet have been inconsistent in advising what a great mission statement might look like. An effective mission statement needs to not only be specific to that organization; it must highlight and focus the energy of everyone in the organization in the direction that the top management team believes is best for the business at that time. If the top management is wrong, then the organization will move quickly and decisively in the wrong direction until new leadership recognizes and corrects the mission. The absence of a mission statement is the missing of the opportunity to communicate. The presence of one poorly done makes the effort to develop one of no value. The core problem is not the presence of a mission statement; it is that far too many are unremarkable, unreadable, too long to remember, and simply not applicable in the daily management of companies.

The culmination of all the studies completed in this area, along with over twenty-five years of assisting companies in the design of effective mission statements, has led to the development of a five-point approach to creating an effective mission statement. These five points should drive the "art" of designing a quality statement.

The Five Keys to Designing a Mission Statement

1. Short: fits on a coffee mug

2. Simple: is something that everyone in the organization can learn and understand

3. Directional: guides every individual in the organization every day

4. Actionable: tells everyone exactly what the organization does and does not do

5. Measurable: can have a metric developed for every part of the statement

Keep It Short

The fun question I ask is, "Does it fit on a coffee mug?" Keeping the statement short may be the single most important element of a well-designed mission statement. The mission statement is not a tome that describes everything that you have done or might do. It most certainly should not be about how you will achieve success in your competitive advantages. It is not written to impress external sources! It is a short, direct statement that can be easily recalled by those within the organization as well as customers, suppliers, and the investing public. Some historic (and not-so-historic) textbook advice that has been around for years has extolled the value of all-encompassing, long mission statements that need to address all of the following elements:[13]

1. customers

2. products/services

3. geographic markets

4. technology

5. concern for survival/growth

6. philosophy

7. public image

8. employees

9. distinctive competence

The result of this advice has been the creation of mission statements that could not be recalled by a poet laureate. An all-encompassing mission statement that cannot be easily recalled by your employees is simply an exercise in frustration, expense, and outright derision. The focus of the statement has to be the succinct expression of the organization's true competitive advantages.

---

13   F.R. David and F.R. David, "It's Time to Redraft Your Mission Statement," *Journal of Business Strategy* 24, no. 1 (2003): 11–14; R.D. Ireland and M.A. Hitt, "Mission Statements: Importance, Challenge, and Recommendations for Development," *Business Horizons* 35, no. 3 (1992): 34–42; J.A. Pearce and F.R. David, "Corporate Mission Statements: The Bottom Line," *Academy of Management Executive* 1, no. 2 (1987): 109–116.

Keep It Simple

A well-designed mission statement has to be something that everyone in the organization can learn *and* understand. A mission statement not well understood and communicated has little if any value to the organization. Spending countless hours crafting a statement only to have it poorly communicated or not reinforced by the senior management of the organization also prevents all the constituents (inside and outside the organization) from knowing the chosen direction of the organization.

The senior management team needs to ensure that the words and concepts employed in the statement have a clear meaning to all who hear or read them. (If you saw the movie *Pirates of the Caribbean*, you may recall the entertaining language play where Captain Barbosa replies tongue in cheek to his upper-class captive, "I'm disinclined to acquiesce to your request," pauses for moment, turns back to his captive and says, "Means '*no*.'") A good mission statement will avoid using adjectives or descriptive language about how the organization will accomplish its mission. An effective mission statement is a guide, not a detailed set of instructions.

Keep It Directional

The mission has to be able to guide every individual in the organization each and every day. It takes extraordinary care to develop a statement that guides the entire organization. Yet, for it to be effectively utilized by every member of the organization, it must have direct applicability to even the most entry-level employee. Imagine the customer service employee who deals with customers calling in with their concerns, complaints, etc. If the mission statement of the organization is a long-winded run of concepts that fundamentally says, "We do it all," or if it is like so many mission statements and simply extols the employees to "maximize shareholder value," then what is the customer service employee to do? What generally happens is that employees simply try to do their best given some mix between their own sense of "justice" and the admonishments of their immediate superior. A well-written statement provides a guidepost for all employees to use when there is a disagreement, there is a set of potential options, dealing with customers, etc.

Keep It Actionable

In order for a mission statement to have direct, measurable impact, it has to be something that helps employees make active decisions in the moment without having to refer every decision up the chain of command. A well-developed mission statement helps ensure that everyone in the organization is heading in the same relative direction so that decisions will not be made counter to the direction that senior management has chosen (with some variance). One mission statement that simultaneously achieves all four components that we have discussed is the one for Southwest Airlines. In it they actually define what they mean by customer service.

Southwest Airlines (2014)

"The mission of Southwest Airlines is dedication to the highest quality of customer service delivered with a sense of warmth, friendliness, individual pride, and organization spirit."

One of the primary goals of an effective mission statement is its ability to allow or even empower employees at all levels to use their judgment in the execution of their daily responsibilities. An effective mission statement tells everyone exactly what they *do* and therefore, by definition, what they *do not do*.

Employees are constantly faced with decisions that appear to be of little importance, but those decisions do indeed have both individual and cumulative impact. An actionable mission statement keeps everyone in the organization actively striving to reinforce the competitive advantages of the organization. The focus within the mission statement goes beyond a laundry list of areas covered in the business; instead, it should be narrowly defined by the means with which the organization succeeds (has advantages that draw customers past competitors). Consider the following:

Autoliv (2014)

"To create, manufacture, and sell state-of-the-art automotive safety systems"

We know exactly what Autoliv will and will not do. If an employee is approached with an interesting new product that will improve the sound quality within the automobile, the employee knows instantly that this is outside the purview of the organization. The senior management has made the decision to focus their time, energy, and resources on the creation, manufacture, and sales of state-of-the-art automotive safety systems. This focus prevents the organization from wasting valuable time and resources pursuing areas outside of their core competence.

Keep It Measurable

The mission statement is only as valuable as it is practical. While all corporations have or should have a set of metrics for the organization, the metrics developed from an effective mission statement focus the organization's efforts on its set of competitive advantages. A great check on the quality of the mission statement that you have written is your ability to design metrics that measure each and every part of the mission. Consider the following mission statement:

New York Times (2014)

"Enhance society by creating, collecting, and distributing high-quality news, information, and entertainment."

This well-designed mission statement allows for the development of metrics that will provide an effective measure of their success at achieving their mission. The *New*

York Times aims to do three things (create, collect, and distribute) across three areas (high-quality news, information, and entertainment) in order to accomplish one goal (enhance society). All of these can then be translated into specific metrics given top management's approach to what constitutes high quality. Examples might be as follows:

1. Number of news articles written by NY Times staff writers that are cited by other news sources divided by the total number of news articles appearing in the NY Times. This could be defined and measured daily.

2. Perception of the quality of articles in the NY Times as evidenced by number of award nominations.

3. Number of NY Times articles that run over multiple days (because of the depth of coverage).

The metrics designed for the NY Times will be unique to that organization and truly measure how it is succeeding in its mission.

Well-Designed Mission Statements

Warby Parker (2019): "To offer designer eyewear at a revolutionary price, while leading the way for socially conscious businesses"

Honest Tea (2019): "To create and promote great-tasting, healthy, organic beverages"

Prezi (2019): "To reinvent how people share knowledge, tell stories, and inspire their audiences to act"

Tesla (2019): "To accelerate the world's transition to sustainable energy"

Nordstrom (2019): "To give customers the most compelling shopping experience possible"

Merck (2019): "To discover, develop, and provide innovative products and services that save and improve lives around the world"

Dow Chemical (2019): "To passionately create innovation for our stakeholders at the intersection of chemistry, biology, and physics"

Nike (2019): "To bring inspiration and innovation to every athlete in the world"

Starbucks (2019): "To inspire and nurture the human spirit—one person, one cup, and one neighborhood at a time"

Poorly Designed Mission Statements

American Standard Organization (2019): "Be the best in the eyes of our customers, employees and shareholders"

Be the best at what? Payroll? What do they produce? Why should we buy from them?

Barnes & Noble (2019): "Our mission is to operate the best specialty retail business in America, regardless of the product we sell. Because the product we sell is books, our aspirations must be consistent with the promise and the ideals of the volumes which line our shelves. To say that our mission exists independent of the product we sell is to demean the importance and the distinction of being booksellers."

Oh my. It is too long. They say they sell anything, then say books. Do books have "ideals"? And if so, what are they? The whole last sentence says nothing.

Chevron (2019): "At the heart of The Chevron Way is our Vision to be the global energy organization most admired for its people, partnership and performance."

Is this a mission or vision? Admired by whom? Whom would you hire or partner with using this mission?

Cooper Tire & Rubber Organization (2019): "The purpose of the Cooper Tire & Rubber Organization is to earn money for its shareholders and increase the value of their investment. We will do that through growing the organization, controlling assets and properly structuring the balance sheet, thereby increasing EPS, cash flow, and return on invested capital."

Well at least they are clear. They are here to make money. They will do that by doing what every other organization on earth does. If they just do all these orthodox things, they will earn money. Notice that there is nothing about what they produce or why any customer should give them money.

Vision

Once a mission statement is in place, many leadership teams turn their attention to where they hope the organization might be in the much longer term. Whereas a mission is very specific and tied directly to the competitive advantages of the organization as it exists today and in the near future, the vision of an organization is intended to be inspirational. Vision statements have a number of common characteristics:

- vivid

- seen/felt/heard

- inspiring

- appeals to emotions

• CEO driven

- describes *where we want to go*

- needs to have a tight focus

- about *behaviors*

While vision statements can be very descriptive, most are succinct and geared toward something very memorable that will inspire people to want to be associated with the organization. The vision should tie back to the competitive advantages of the organization such that those advantages help the organization strive toward the vision. The vision is not meant to be 100 percent achievable but getting closer and closer is motivating.

Evaluation of the effectiveness of a vision statement is very much in the eye of the beholder. Whereas a mission is very concrete and guides actions on a daily basis, the vision is open to wide interpretation. What inspires one set of employees might seem inconsequential to another set of employees. The goal of all of these efforts is to get employees all moving in generally the same direction. The more latitude of interpretation in the vision statement, the more likely that employee efforts will be widely dispersed (defeating the whole purpose of crafting one).

Consider the following vision statements and my observations on each:

Alzheimer's Association: "A world without Alzheimer's"

This is a very tight approach that might mean efforts in many areas within the organization that counter and compete, but it has everyone aimed in a single direction.

Save the Children: "A world in which every child attains the right to survival, protection, development, and participation"

Once again, this is focused on a single area (children) while widening the arc of attention into four different areas. One just hopes that the structure of the organization is tied to this.

The Walt Disney Organization: "To make people happy"

It's hard to miss the desire here. There are so many interactions with customers every day that any addition to this would just muddy the message.

ArcelorMittal: "To be the most admired steel producer in the world: a benchmark for the global steel industry"

Not sure what "most admired" is, but the organization is going to be a steel producer for the long haul. Not very inspiring.

Valero: "Will be the premier manufacturer, distributor and marketer of quality transportation fuels and petrochemical feedstocks, while serving the needs of our employees, communities and stakeholders"

Just doesn't say anything that would be even slightly inspiring. Appears to be a laundry list of areas in which they operate. Ridiculously generic with employees, communities, and stakeholders. What else is there?

Coca-Cola: "Our vision serves as the framework for our Roadmap and guides every aspect of our business by describing what we need to accomplish in order to continue achieving sustainable, quality growth.

People: Be a great place to work where people are inspired to be the best they can be.

Portfolio: Bring to the world a portfolio of quality beverage brands that anticipate and satisfy people's desires and needs.

Partners: Nurture a winning network of customers and suppliers, together we create mutual, enduring value.

Planet: Be a responsible citizen that makes a difference by helping build and support sustainable communities.

Profit: Maximize long-term return to shareowners while being mindful of our overall responsibilities.

Productivity: Be a highly effective, lean and fast-moving organization."

Oh my! This is just painful. It's too long for anyone to remember anything past the six Ps. Some elements are counter to each other. Mostly it is just a bunch of words where virtually anyone can find something that they like and move forward on that. If the goal of a vision is to inspire in a single direction, Coca-Cola has people running every different direction.

Kraft Heinz: "To be the best food organization, growing a better world"

Not sure what "best" is. The focus is so wide that virtually any action can be taken. Some might interpret this as non-GMO, others as

organic, others as they should get out of the packaging business and
be in farming. The list goes on.

Values/Principles

An organization trying to implement virtually any strategy must have the active cooperation of its employees. Employees work for far more than a paycheck and benefits. They want to work where they feel good about their contribution to the overall efforts of the organization (or research suggests that this is the case for most employees). Organizations have values, even when they are not codified, that are apparent to everyone inside an organization (and sometimes outside as well). Codified value statements are designed to send a message to customers, suppliers, potential employees, and other stakeholders about what will be expected and, sometimes, what is not going to be tolerated.

Strict management adherence to these principles is critical for management to guide employees. A token effort or even outright violation of stated values brings nothing but derision.

There is not a "correct" set of values, nor is there a standard methodology/limit to the number. Some examples of value statements from the companies that we have discussed above in mission/vision include the following:

Warby Parker (2019)

Treat customers the way we'd like to be treated. They don't call it the golden rule for nothing. Shopping for glasses should be fun, easy, and not ridiculously expensive.

Create an environment where employees can think big, have fun, and do good. Sometimes people say to us: "If you love your job so much, why don't you marry it?" (Answer: we would if we could.)

Get out there. No organization is an island. Serving the community is in our DNA—from distributing a pair of frames for every pair sold to sponsoring local Little League teams (Go Giants! Go Skyscrapers!). We also work with Verité to ensure that our factories have fair working conditions and happy employees.

Green is good. Warby Parker is one of the only carbon-neutral eyewear brands in the world.

Prezi (2019)

We picture. Because visual thinking allows us to be more creative. We use it to understand each other and solve problems more effectively.

We care. Because change only happens when we support the people who expand our horizons, we act and lead by example in our closer and wider communities.

We team. Because together we are greater than the sum of our parts, we build our team on the foundations of trust and transparency.

Tesla (2019)

Always do your best. We endeavor to apply the brightest minds and the best available technology to each and every new challenge. We do not cut corners, and we do not settle.

No forecast is perfect but try anyway. We constantly strive to improve the accuracy of our forecasts as well as the reliability and service with which they are delivered.

Respect and encourage people. We believe that our companies are only as successful as our clients and team members are successful. Treating them with respect and encouraging their success is the surest way to encourage the companies' success.

Always be learning. The world in which we live and the industry in which we operate are constantly changing. It is imperative to both personal and professional success that we understand those changes and adapt accordingly.

Respect the environment. We believe that our efforts to help the energy industry achieve greater efficiencies help ease the strain that humans put on the environment.

The Coca-Cola Organization

Leadership: The courage to shape a better future

Collaboration: Leverage collective genius

Integrity: Be real

Accountability: If it is to be, it's up to me

Passion: Committed in heart and mind

Diversity: As inclusive as our brands

Quality: What we do, we do well

The overall point of this chapter is to begin the process of implementation with the most overarching methods of communicating. While there are many forms of communication, and most of the remaining chapters in this book discuss varying means of communicating, it all starts with a clear foundation. Mission, vision, and values set the course for all of the remaining work in strategy implementation.

Chapter 8

How to Measure Success— Metrics and Fit

Well-designed mission/vision/value statements are part of the foundation of implanting the strategy with employees in the organization. Before moving on to the other elements of implementation, it is crucial that the organization determine what will constitute success and be very clear about how it will be measured. Setting this out at the beginning of the strategy implementation effort ensures understanding by everyone involved and establishes the baseline means of measuring that success.

Metrics are one of the elements of the one-page strategy map, and they must tie directly to the competitive advantages of the organization. It is important to understand the process, what constitutes an effective strategy metric, why it is not an outcome measure, and how we use metrics to drive performance in the organization.

Nothing works quite so well as a well-crafted "organization activity scorecard."

Strategy metrics are designed to both guide and demonstrate that the activities of employees are reinforcing the competitive strategy. In our effort to implement strategy, we are not trying to measure classic accounting or financial metrics of performance. Those will be measured and should be measured, but they are lagging variables that are a result of the activities by employees. Leadership needs to not only be clear about what activities they believe will lead to the success of the organization, but also how they will measure those activities. Once again, it is critical that we get past concept activities ("treat customers as your family," "be innovative," "do the right thing," "safety first," etc.) and be very specific about the activities that we believe will be most influential in driving our competitive advantages.

All of this effort is aligned around the concept of *fit* within the organization. There should be consistency and alignment between what we believe makes the business unique and how that is perceived by customers. Every activity that is measured should reinforce the specific strategy that the organization is trying to drive.

Sure, we want profits to rise, customer traffic to increase, customer turnover to go down, and complaints to go down (among others), but we can't just tell employees to make it happen. Tell the person in charge of cooking the French fries at a fast-food restaurant that we need to increase sales by 6 percent, and they will just stare at you! What one employee might believe would work well might exactly counter what another employee believes would work well. Employees perform activities for the business that, if guided correctly and consistently, will lead to positive post hoc measures of performance such as those above.

While all tied together, there are a number of unique elements that should be considered in the design of strategy metrics:

1.   type of metrics

       a) qualitative versus quantitative

       b) activity versus outcome

2.   tie to strategy

3.   use of pre- and post-measurement

4.   raw numbers, mean, range, continuous, discrete, and goal metrics

5.   collinearity

6.   big data

Type of Metrics—Qualitative versus Quantitative

There is a fairly compelling argument made by many people that if you can't quantify it, then you can't measure it. Quantitative data gathering and analysis is a critical part of determining that desired activities are being completed. However, there is a place in strategy implementation where understanding is best gained by the depth and context associated with the use of qualitative metrics.

Quantitative metrics:	Those measures represented by some type of observable data
Qualitative metrics:	Information gathered that is contextual in nature, representing nonnumerical measures

Quantitative metrics are the measures or results that virtually everyone is most comfortable reporting and considering. Outcome (not activity-based strategy) metrics might include the number of unique visits to our website, the percentage of customers purchasing more than one item, the average time for a new customer to enroll in our loyalty program, and so on. There is something quite reassuring about being able to identify a result and compare it directly to the result from the previous day, week, quarter, or year.

Qualitative metrics include the perceptions of employees, customers, and government agencies about the activities and business model of the organization. Reputation is a qualitative measure often seen in the organization's ability to influence others. The work-life feel of an organization improves its ability to attract and retain employees. While many organizations offer similar benefits, some have a different "feel" that is nonquantifiable. It is tempting to find a way to quantify even these loose elements; however, they have unique value as relative measures and should be allowed to be a basis of discussion and "feel" in the organization.

Quantifiable metrics alone provide insufficient information from which to make strategy decisions. An insidious issue that is often overlooked is the method by which the metric has been calculated. There is significant manipulation of most metrics (even the ones we think we understand well); therefore, the only real value in most metrics is not in the measure itself but in its comparison with the previous period. The delta (change) in the metric becomes a barometer of success.

Consider the reporting of same-store sales. The raw number is far less important than the change from the previous year. Every location has unique issues and customers. The change from the previous year helps organizations balance those issues and look at the improvement at the store level (or any more precise level of analysis). Strategists are particularly interested in comparison and change metrics. It is irrelevant to learn that sales went up by 3.4 percent without the context of what happened previously in your own operation or in comparison to your competitors. If the competition went up 8 percent, then the 3.4 percent looks terrible.

Quantitative metrics are of real value to a business; however, they only provide snapshots of information to the management team. In order to get a more complete look at the business, managers keep adding and adding quantitative metrics to their reporting. One report begets another, and the IT department staffs up to provide more and more "results" in so-called readable forms for management to evaluate the state of the organization. It is a never-ending cycle that needs to be curbed. We will discuss several techniques for the drastic reduction of data collection when we talk about collinearity later in this chapter.

Qualitative metrics provide us the opportunity to fill context and understanding in between the quantitative metrics. This is especially important as we reduce the raw number of snapshot quantitative metrics that are reported. The real difficulty lies in preventing the quantification of everything collected.

How do you gauge what a particular customer thinks about the French fries at McDonald's versus Burger King versus Wendy's? We can ask customers to rank various aspects of our French fries, but we may not be getting at why they prefer (or don't prefer) our French fries. Listening to how customers describe the fries, what they don't like about the fries, and how they feel about the fries provides a depth of understanding not easily applicable to quantification.

Developing a feel for the qualitative aspects of the business can be done in a number of ways. In the early years of his business, J. Peterman held a breakfast with eight to ten different employees every week. His only rule about what could be discussed was that there were no rules. Alan Mullaly regularly sat in the back of various meetings to get a sense of how the business was progressing. It takes a hands-on approach to collect qualitative input.

Some companies hire consultants to run focus groups with customers, test the market for new ideas, and watch consumer and employee behavior. Requiring every senior manager to work the customer service lines for eight hours a quarter is a quantitative metric that will lead to spectacular qualitative insights. We can easily poke fun at shows like *Undercover Boss*, but the lack of insight into the jobs that actually make the money for an organization points out how quickly one can lose touch (if they ever even had touch). A method for collecting and utilizing qualitative data is a means for staying ahead of the competition.

All this is to encourage a mix between qualitative and quantitative metric collection. The reality is that we can combine the two to provide unique insights. Using techniques such as content analysis or conjoint analysis allows unique insights for use by the leadership team.

Type of Metrics—Outcome versus Activity

Virtually everyone in every organization is very familiar with the many outcome measures used to evaluate success:

- sales

- expense ratio

- net income

- profit margin

- productivity

- net promoter score (simply one of the most poorly designed and statistically flawed outcome measures ever created)

- same-store sales

- inventory turnover

- returns

These types of metrics are quite valuable, but they provide information only on the outcomes of the organization. How did these outcomes change from one period to the next? What if they did not change the way that leadership was hoping for? What levers should the leadership team push to move them forward? What is preventing the organization from achieving its goals?

Leadership is about crafting an informed hypothesis about success and ensuring that the activities of employees are directed to move that hypothesis forward.

All organizations operate under management hypotheses! That is, a leadership team believes that if employees do X, Y, and Z, then the organization will see increased sales, profits, etc. It is not a *"known"* (if it were, then every leadership team would know exactly what would yield them the results they are looking for); it is a hypothesis that takes into account all of the elements of the business, the competition, and the environment in which it operates. Once this is established, the next step is to determine whether employees are actually doing what we believe will lead to our success. Are they focusing their efforts on the organization's competitive advantages? Therefore, in strategy implementation, these quantifiable metrics must be about the *activities* that we want employees to do.

Tie to Strategy

Strategy is a journey over a period of time. For strategy to mean anything beyond the words on a page, it has to be measured, and adjustments must be made in those measures to direct employees to do what needs to be done. As stated earlier, the metrics used must examine the activities, not the results, that we believe will move us closer to knowing that our strategy is actually being implemented.

I have spoken with many CEOs who are frustrated that their well-designed strategy has not led to the organization growth they had envisioned. With a bit of investigation, we find that we can't evaluate the success or failure of the strategy because it was never really implemented. Management teams below senior management paid lip service to the new direction but didn't change any of their actions.

Companies need a completely new set of metrics to know that the strategy is actually being implemented. Those activity metrics need to be tied directly to the unique strategy (competitive advantages) of the business.

STRATEGY	METRICS
Most convenient	Number of minutes it takes to move a vehicle from curbside drop- off to offsite parking (thus freeing up curbside parking and making it more appealing to customers): number of minutes from vehicle arrival at curbside to return of attendant to curbside (evaluated daily or hourly)
	Time to initial greeting of customer (makes the customer feel that they are being taken care of): number of seconds from customer arrival to initial greeting (evaluated daily)
	Number of clicks required by the customer to purchase (reduction in clicks makes it easier): number of clicks actually made by customers from initial website entry to completed transaction / evaluated daily
	Number of dedicated sales staff (ability to reach a salesperson easily): number of dedicated salespeople divided by total number of customers
	How up-to-date employees are on the latest customer service initiatives (improves the consistency of delivery to customers): number of in-store employees attending refresher trainings divided by total number of employees

STRATEGY	METRICS
Best available selection	Number of items available for purchase when ordered (makes it the go-to place for customers—would like to see the number of specialty items ordered go down at least "to a point"): number of specialty orders divided by total number of orders
	Number of times employees are able to resolve an issue about a customer not finding what they are looking for (gives customers confidence): number of daily resolved customer complaints on being unable to find products divided by total daily complaints on being unable to find products
	Having everything that the customer needs to complete a particular project: number of items on-hand to complete a project divided by number of projects that items can be used for by customers
	Number of products available during certain hours (customers operating outside standard hours might look for full selection): number of items available to customers after midnight divided by number of items available to customers before midnight
Highest expertise	Number of times an employee must refer to outside sources to answer a customer question (provide customers with confidence): number of times an employee refers to an outside source divided by number of questions received by customers

STRATEGY	METRICS
	Number of employees who have completed industry certifications (outside certifications provide validation): number of employees who have completed industry certifications divided by total number of employees
	Number of articles/presentations made by employees to outside groups (shows off current expertise and provides visibility as an organization known as an expert): number of published articles or industry presentations per year divided by total number of employees
Personal connection	Number of customers about whom employees can recall at least five important personal elements (knowing personal information and ability to recall it provides a connection with customers): number of customers about whom employees can recall at least five important personal elements divided by number of employees
	Percentage of time an employee knows customers' orders before they order (there's nothing that regular customers appreciate more): number of customer orders stated by employee before the customer actually tries to order divided by total orders (per hour/day/month)
	Number of customers contacted after an order to determine satisfaction with no additional sales pitch (customers generally appreciate not just being an order): number of customers contacted

after ordering solely to determine if anything else can be done divided by total number of customers (per day/month/quarter)

Note that not only are these activity metrics, but they are also all aimed toward the actions of employees that will impact the perceptions or responses of paying customers. If designed effectively, the change that the strategy envisions will result in a change in employee actions. All of the metrics can be used at an organization level as well as the individual employee level.

We worked with a nonprofit organization that (among other competitive advantages) had a competitive advantage of going out to the client instead of having the client come to them for services. It passed RBA relative to the other nonprofit organizations in their community. We crafted a metric: number of visits outside office divided by total visits with clients.

When we measured this against performance, we found that the mean was roughly 91 percent. This made sense, since some clients simply preferred to come to the office. However, when we dug deeper into this number, we found three counselors in the organization with percentages below 50 percent. Each was approached and questioned about how low this number was for them. Each expressed a reluctance to meet clients outside the office (uncomfortable, inconvenient, ego, etc.). The reality was that they were not delivering on the strategy promise.

In order for strategy implementation to be effective, it must be consistently delivered. If you tell a customer (client) that they should buy from your organization (or use your organization, if nonprofit) because you do X, Y, and Z that make your offering rare, durable, relatively nonsubstitutable, nontradable, and valuable, then *you must deliver on the promise!* Every time an employee does not deliver on the promises made, the customer discounts the message being delivered and considers alternatives.

Use of Pre- and Postmeasurement

There is a very effective saying that I use on a regular basis with organizations:

"You are what you are."

The organization may have pitched itself as the most caring, most accurate, highest quality organization in the industry, when it actually falls quite short on all of those aspects. All organizations exist in the market today with reputations, customers, employees, and capabilities. The senior management may wish that the organization was viewed as more innovative, cohesive, collaborative, or any of a host of concepts. However, accepting where the organization is today is a great place to set the baseline for all metrics.

We worked with a large manufacturing organization where the leadership team proudly proclaimed that it had a 92 percent on-time delivery record. This would have been a remarkable competitive advantage in their industry, as the mean for the industry was roughly 68 percent. While working with a group of middle managers on their competitive advantages, I pushed the group to look at the processes that allowed this type of remarkable on-time delivery record.

The senior management of the organization wanted to use that 92 percent as the baseline and look to increase it to 94 percent within a year in order to maintain their sizable lead over the competitors. The middle managers kept pushing back on using this as a competitive advantage, when one manager finally shared the following (paraphrased from the original):

"Well, Chuck, it really may not be 92 percent. See, if we have a problem with manufacturing, supply, delivery, or anything really, then we call the customer and let them know about the problem and reset the delivery date with their permission."

"What do you do if the customer does not give you permission?" I asked.

"Haha, well...we change it anyway because we have an issue."

"OK, then why is your on-time rate not 100 percent?" I posed to the group.

There was a long delay with a lot of murmuring; then the answer finally came: "Guess we figured that senior management would not believe that number."

I went back to senior management, and we decided to shut down their ability to make changes to the scheduled delivery date once it had been entered into the system (no small feat, as IT thought we had asked for Neptune and Saturn to be switched in the solar system). After a month, it became clear that the on-time delivery record was going to be very bad. At the three-month mark, we concluded that the real on-time delivery percentage was 8 percent.

As dejecting as that was for the senior management to deal with, strategy metrics are about accepting where you are and improving on that. We set 8 percent as the baseline and started measuring performance from there. Initially, the senior management demanded that on-time delivery double (to 16 percent) within three months. This may not sound spectacular, but this metric was so far below the median in the industry—if we presume that all the other competitors were telling the truth—that it was not a potential competitive advantage (as they had hoped) but a standard operation (orthodox) that was well below the industry expectations. The reality was that customers knew this already and had complained for many years. The company had lost business because of this, and yet leadership continued to tell themselves that it was not the case, that those customers were just being unreasonable. They even cited an instance (only one, mind you) where a customer came back because of even worse on-time performance by a competitor (it seems to be a common practice in business to extrapolate from a single instance or a few instances and argue that it is the norm).

You must establish premeasurements for all strategy metrics that you design. Then set regular time periods for evaluation of each metric, and report those results. What strategists most care about in this instance is the change (delta) in the metric. We are looking for continuous improvement in all of our activity metrics, and ultimately, we should see those tie to improvement in classic post hoc metrics for the organization.

Raw Numbers, Mean, Range, Continuous, Discrete, and Goal Metrics

There are some very common approaches to strategy metrics that need to be discussed. The classic approach used by far too many folks is to examine the overall company average (mean) or some type of raw number count as a means for tracking activity improvement. Unfortunately, both of these have significant flaws that can be easily manipulated, preventing management from gaining the improvements that they are seeking. It is important to understand the value and contribution to employee performance provided by using a variety of metrics.

Utilizing **raw numbers** as an activity metric is the single biggest mistake that can be made. Organizations grow and change over time, and the value of the raw number to the actual experience of the customer can easily get distorted. We can see the number of calls answered within five seconds grow month over month by 3 percent. What we don't see is that overall call growth was growing by 8 percent. Thus the average customer was seeing fewer instances where their call was answered within 5 seconds. Raw numbers distort activities.

While all metrics have inherent issues, overall organization averages (**means**) do a particular disservice to the organization, because improvements in the measure may be achieved by reducing the denominator (number of behaviors tracked) or by increasing the numerator (desired behavior). Overall organizational averages must use denominators that directly relate to customer interactions and perceptions. You will note that a good activity metric that has both a numerator and a denominator is not only used to look at the overall organization, but also to evaluate the specific performance of every employee.

Range as a metric allows us to look at the improvement in the consistency of the experience of the customer. We worked with a small restaurant operation that had a drive-in line. Senior management carefully monitored the speed with which each customer was served. The goal was to keep the average wait to no more than four minutes. However, a one-hour watch of the drive-in line found that customers experienced a range of performance that ran from virtually instant service (items ready when they rolled up to the window) to waiting fifteen minutes before being served. Inconsistency in *any* experience that a customer receives from your organization is a source of frustration. Consistency (as I've pointed out before) is a key to strategy success.

Consider what might have happened to the customer over ten contacts with the organization:

Customer contact	1	2	3	4	5	6	7	8	9	10	AVG
Wait time to service (sec)	0	0	15	35	50	180	180	255	810	820	234.5

Now, imagine that a huge effort was made by senior management to get employees to improve the average wait time for the customer. The result might be as follows:

Customer contact	1	2	3	4	5	6	7	8	9	10	AVG
Wait time to service (sec)	0	0	0	20	70	75	75	265	905	910	232

The result was a slight decrease in the average wait time for the customer over ten visits (something that might have resulted in applause and bonuses). There was improvement in the number of times that the customer waited less than four minutes; however, the actual times when they missed the four-minute mark grew significantly in length.

Interviews with the employees delivering the experience revealed that they felt they knew that what management really cared about was the number of times that a customer waited for less than four minutes. Once a customer had not been helped within that window, employees simply pushed them out of the queue and sent them to a special parking spot to await their order while trying to maximize the numbers that they could serve within the desired window of time.

Range is a far more important metric in strategy than mean. Reducing the range of wait times that customers experience (regardless of whether the average goes up or down) allows senior management to be more confident in the consistency of implementation of the strategy. It also provides a window into activities that could reduce the range.

Continuous and **discrete** measures of strategy allow for very different results from employees. Discrete metrics are those taken at points in time. They allow senior management to hold a number of extraneous factors constant while examining the movement of the metric being examined. Employees generally know when measures are being taken, and even with no malice intended, they adjust their performance. Discrete measures are of some value, but they should be used in combination with continuous measures. If we assume that an organization can always improve (a fairly safe assumption), then we don't want employees to stop striving or varying their efforts. Continuous measures have no upward bound. You will notice that all the measures listed earlier in the chapter lend themselves to continuous measurement.

Goal metrics are a unique element within strategy implementation. Any part of the business that is standard operations (orthodox) should have a goal established. Remember that, by definition, its operation and measurement are simply expected (and known) in the industry. We do not seek to be above the median expectation in anything orthodox; therefore, it is appropriate to establish a goal. Once that goal is achieved, we simply want to maintain it. Goals are not appropriate for areas where we are trying to achieve a competitive advantage. We want to go as far as possible with these advantages, and therefore all competitive advantages should be measured with continuous metrics.

Big Data and Collinearity

Developing a set of activity metrics for the business is an important step, and inevitably, the business will collect a vast array of activity metrics. We've worked with a number of businesses that had an initial list of activity metrics that ran from thirty-six to over fifty! Every tracked metric seems to have a sponsor within the organization who simply could not live without that particular piece of information. Yet we all realize that there are too many data points tracked in general. Added to this issue is the drive toward collecting and evaluating "big data" by so many organizations that seem to believe that if they can just slice up all the data available to the business, then executives will be provided with "answers" that will help them grow the organization. Let's address each of these.

Big data as a strategy driver has many fallacies inherently built into the concept. The first is the issue of population data. Many executives seem to believe that if they use all the data collected by the organization, they will find insights not available by using classic statistical estimation techniques. While there is an extremely small chance that this is true, it is far outweighed by the sheer cost associated with collecting, holding, managing, analyzing, and reporting the analysis. The chances of an error of estimation can be reduced to an extraordinarily small number with classical sampling.

However, the biggest misconception is that these companies are really working with population data in the first place. Companies do not collect population data; they can only collect data from the population of the organization's customers. It has a bias built in that provides no insight into what your competitors' customers are doing. As such, saving the expense and effort of trying to analyze millions or tens of millions of transactions is even more justified.

biased data collection

There can be real value in analyzing organization "big data"; however, that analysis needs to be focused on the desired strategy elements of the business and needs to take into consideration the cost and time of such huge efforts. The rest is just noise.

Statistical techniques with a well-developed database of observations yields results that can be within a very, very tight range of the actual situation. Using just a sampling of data developed with some precision as to selection, it is relatively easy to be 99 percent confident in your results.

The other issue is one of reducing the amount of information collected, analyzed, and reported in organizations. What is the quickest and most reliable means of reducing the number of metrics being tracked? A Pearson correlation table provides insights

131

into how relatable each metric is to each other. Without going into vast detail about the workings of the approach, suffice it to say that a Pearson correlation table (available in any spreadsheet package) will compare every metric you track to every other metric.

Two metrics that are perfectly correlated (that is, they move together in lockstep) will have a value of 1.0 (this is rarely, if ever, seen). Two metrics that are perfectly correlated in the opposite direction will have a value of -1.0 (also rarely seen). The table will be filled with values that lie between 1.0 and -1.0 (obviously any metric is perfectly and positively correlated with itself). For our purposes and for being able to use metrics in some type of predictive analysis for activities related to strategy, any number greater than 0.4 or less than -0.4 means that those two metrics are so highly correlated that they are effectively measuring the same thing (this is just a rule of thumb for the purposes of strategy implementation).

	Mean	s.d.	1	2	3	4	5	6	7	8	9	10	11	12	13	14	15	16
1.	203	53	1.00															
2.	.00	1.00	.01	1.00														
3.	3.41	1.44	.10	-.56	1.00													
4.	7.45	3.56	.24	-.18	.04	1.00												
5.	.26	.17	.05	-.47	-.20	.12	1.00											
6.	.62	.40	.02	.10	.02	.03	.02	1.00										
7.	.00	1.00	-.07	-.49	-.09	-.01	.26	.01	1.00									
8.	3.63	1.88	.22	-.05	.41	.13	-.07	.19	-.07	1.00								
9.	8.09	3.57	.23	-.16	.04	.72	.10	.06	.01	.23	1.00							
10.	.10	.06	-.01	-.13	-.02	-.01	.14	-.01	.21	-.01	-.01	1.00						
11.	4.37	1.23	.01	-.67	.01	-.06	.17	.35	.59	.07	-.06	-.02	1.00					
12.	3392	2450	.32	-.64	.20	.29	.21	.23	-.55	.48	.26	.11	.24	1.00				
13.	1982	1.09	.12	-.13	-.09	.05	.11	.02	.06	.03	.09	.10	.06	.30	1.00			
14.	14.68	1.88	.23	-.21	.08	.25	.11	.21	.13	.26	.23	.02	.04	.37	.03	1.00		
15.	.0051	.0087	.11	-.08	.04	.08	.02	-.02	.02	.01	.13	-.02	-.01	.15	.08	.04	1.00	
16.	4690	174	-.05	.02	-.03	.13	.02	.05	-.02	.03	.13	-.09	-.02	-.09	-.20	-.33	-.01	1.00

Take a look at the table above. After all the metrics are collected for a period of time (one month in this case), every metric is evaluated against every other metric with this very straightforward statistical look. The "1.00" down the diagonal simply confirms that every variable is perfectly correlated with itself. The highlighted correlations are ones that exceed our .4/-.4 threshold. These metrics are so highly related that they effectively measure the same thing. In these cases, management should choose one to collect and track while eliminating the collection and reporting of the other. Our rule of thumb is to collect the metric that is easiest to obtain and understand.

In this example:

1. Metric 2 is highly negatively correlated with metrics 3, 7, 11, and 12.

2. Metric 4 is highly positively correlated with metric 9.

3. Not surprisingly, metric 7 is highly positively correlated with metrics 11 and 12.

Collecting metric 2 allows us to eliminate the collection of three other metrics while keeping in mind that those metrics move in the opposite direction from metric 2. We could collect either metric 4 or metric 9 but should not collect both.

This approach can and should be done over and over throughout the organization's metrics in order to narrow the number collected and to allow management to focus their attention. While there is a lot to consider in the measurement of strategy, the elements that we briefly discussed in this chapter will go a long way toward ensuring that the strategy designed is being measured with activity metrics that provide insight to the senior leadership team.

Chapter 9

Structuring the Organization Sensibly

There is nothing more visible in the implementation of strategy than how we organize the people in the organization who will make that strategy a reality.

Want to shut down most of the work being done on a daily basis in your organization? Just mention that there might be a reorganization. Whom one reports to on a daily basis is a contentious issue in any organization. I have found that people are all-in with developing strategy right up to the point where we start talking about reorganizing the business to align its operations with the new strategy. At that point, management wants to distance itself quickly from the effort. This reluctance comes not only from the nature of reporting to someone new, but also from a long, long history of reorganizations that have "arbitrary" written all over them.

Every manager we talk with seems to have their own approach to how the business should be organized. These approaches are bound in the manager's "theory of the business" and lead to structures that might or might not advance the strategy of the business. When employees don't understand why a structure has been put in place or how it will work with the strategy, then the whole effort is undermined.

The long, hard truth of outstanding organizational performance is that structure follows strategy. Once you have developed your competitive advantages, it is imperative that you structure the business around those advantages. Every single textbook on strategy has a chapter on the forms of structure that are presented (with lovely charts) and describe the meta-approaches to the topic. These include terms such as the following:

1. functional

2. divisional

3. geographic

4. multidomestic

5. network

6. matrix

All of these global approaches describe an overall approach that has little to do with the design and implementation of strategy. They are conceptually correct in their description of reporting relationships, and we will refer back to and utilize these "charts" as a means of displaying the structure after we have aligned the employees in the organization.

Structuring an organization is *hard*, and it takes a lot of work to keep it relevant.

The Goal of Structuring the Organization

To effectively deliver on the strategic differentiation of the organization in a manner that has the fewest possible layers between the CEO and the lowest-level worker

Structure is really just another means of communicating to employees about where their focus should be. As discussed much earlier in this book, communication is one of the limitations to effective strategy implementation. Along with a common purpose, another significant limitation is the willingness of employees to serve the organization. That willingness can vary from totally unwilling (oppose the efforts the leadership is trying to drive) to complete willingness (every effort is aimed at pushing the strategy forward). The employees on these two extremes are the minority in most organizations. Those who are bent on opposing the efforts of leadership (especially in a strategic change situation) should be counseled out of the organization for their own and the organization's good. Those who are fully bought into the strategy need very little additional communication to push the competitive advantages forward.

The majority of employees lie somewhere in the middle in an area referred to as the "zone of indifference." Those employees will implement a strategy for the organization as long as it fits with their view of what the organization does, they believe it will help the organization succeed, it aligns with their ethical framework, and they have trust in the leadership team. The zone of indifference is part of the implicit contract taken out with employees. As long as they are being compensated (in a broad sense of that term), then the employee is there to do the best they can for the organization.

In strategy implementation, our goal is to ensure that all strategic change efforts fall within this zone of indifference for the majority of the employees. As a change in strategy is perceived as testing the bounds on the lower end, the leadership team has to do more and more to convince the employees to do what they want them to do. The more radical the change, the more likely it is to fall outside this zone for employees. A big part of keeping employees within this zone is designing a very logical, fair, and obviously effective structure for the organization to align with the strategy.

Since one of the big goals of structuring an organization is to limit the layers between the leadership and front-line employees, structure must enable each leader to effectively deliver results while directing as many employees as is practical. That simply cannot be accomplished by just adding people to a particular manager. We need a means by which we can effectively direct large numbers of people in the organization.

Henry Mintzberg wrote the most applicable and insightful look at the subject in his book *The Structuring of Organizations*.[14] While there has been a lot of work on this topic since this book, the book stands strong for managers looking for a meaningful way to structure their organization. Once a strategy is in place, a mission has been crafted, and the strategy metrics have been designed, it is incumbent on the managers to structure the business to make the most of this effort. The approach discussed below uses Mintzberg's method as its foundation and incorporates the latest practical knowledge in the field.

---

14   Henry Mintzberg, *The Structuring of Organizations* (Englewood Cliffs, NJ: Prentice Hall, 1979).

With the exception of executive management, every person working in an organization can be categorized as belonging to one of three elements or areas of the business:

1. strategy core

2. in-house advisors and policy makers

3. operations

Each of those areas needs to be coordinated. There are four fundamental approaches, with a fifth that is still being debated. The goal of the coordination method chosen is to maximize the number of employees that can be managed by a single manager or leader while achieving the goals of the organization. The coordination approaches are as follows:

1. mutual team adjustment

2. standardization of work processes

3. standardization of worker skills

4. standardization of work output

5. standardization of business norms (not seen in for-profit organizations)

Three Areas of Any Organization

As we stated above, every individual in an organization can be effectively divided into one of three areas. The *strategy core* is that group or groups most responsible for the competitive advantages of the business. The core needs to have *in-house advisors* (experts) and *policy makers* (protectors). Advisors are specialists who assist the core group or groups as they push the competitive advantages of the business forward. Policy makers protect the organization by ensuring that policies and procedures are in place and are followed as required by regulators, business practices, laws, and the desires of senior managers. The *operations* groups are those charged with most of the standard elements of the business.

There is no perfect way to organize a business, but how it is organized will make a huge difference in its ability to deliver on its stated strategy. Now that we have established the foundations for structuring the organization, let's take a look at a business and contemplate how it might be organized.

Consider a fairly typical fast-food restaurant in the United States. The restaurant has dozens (maybe hundreds) of standard operational elements. It has a counter, tables, chairs, napkins, a cash register, a soda machine, a menu display board, fryers, some type of assembly line for food preparation and cooking, display cases, refrigerators, freezers, trash cans, air conditioning and heating, procedures for preparing food, cleaning requirements, methods of reporting sales and costs, and so on.

As has been discussed a number of times, all of these standard elements of the business need to be done, and done well, but they don't need to be done any better than the competition unless some element is being crafted as a true competitive advantage. We want to supply napkins for our customers, but we only need to supply average napkins. Too high a quality and they will start disappearing in large numbers; too low a quality and customers will complain or never come back. Ketchup is an expectation (at least in the United States), but what quality allows the restaurant to minimize costs without losing sales? These standard elements are critical to the running of the business, but they are not the reason that the customer has chosen this particular fast-food restaurant over the dozens of others.

Every element that was just listed (and many more) is the responsibility of the various operations functions. We want to organize the business such that all the *standard* elements of the business are handled by a group or groups whose entire job is to maintain an acceptable level of performance equal (or close to equal) to that of our direct competitors.

For the sake of this discussion, let's presume that the true competitive advantages of this fast-food restaurant are (1) a 24-7 operation where the customer can have breakfast or regular food items anytime, and (2) a private dining area where no cell phone may be used and no talking is allowed.

In this case, one of the strategy core groups would be focused on the specific requirements of each restaurant in order for it to make every type of food offered twenty-four hours a day. The procedures, logistics, and handling that will ensure that this element of the strategy can be delivered are core to the success of the business (if the leadership is correct about this being a competitive advantage). Another strategy core group would be focused on the design of a private area within each and every location as well as procedures to ensure that it remains true to the offering. Refining and continuous improvement of these two competitive advantages need to be the full-time job of a core group of individuals.

In-house advisors and policy makers round out the design of the business. They play a central role between the standard and the exceptional elements of the business. Advisors might be engineering, mechanical, menu design, logistics, and legal groups, whereas human resources, accounting, and store operations might be logically placed in the policy maker role. Policy makers have the power to protect the organization by setting appropriate policies and providing the organization with consistency, whereas advisors provide specialized information and expertise within the organization to help the core make better decisions. The reason that these two groups are bound together is that there is crossover in each group's responsibilities. There are groups such as accounting where part of the function is to provide advice, whereas another part of the function would be to establish hard and fast policies. It is important to separate these groups within the function so that the role of each is well understood in the sider organization. Policy makers have the power to establish procedures that the rest of the organization must follow while advice givers are just that—they provide advice that the core can chose to accept or reject.

Virtually any group can be categorized as operations, in-house advisors, or in-house policy makers. The way you craft which group falls into which category determines their roles in the organization and completely changes the focus of the organization. As was stated before, there is no "right" way to structure an organization; however, by applying a bit of the "science" of strategy, you can establish a focus on the elements that truly differentiate the organization.

Let's return to a restaurant example, but this time make the restaurant a mid-priced, suburban operation catering to families desiring to eat out casually in the evenings. If we craft the operation with the cooks as the core, then the business quickly develops a focus on the quality and consistency of the food presentation. The food might take longer to get to the table, but the cooks in the kitchen are core, and therefore it is their operation that drives the functioning. Hopefully this restaurant has made the food selection, consistency, freshness, etc. a stated advantage.

You could organize the exact same restaurant with the wait staff as core. The operation would be focused on quick service, and the waitstaff would drive what the business made in the kitchen. The waitstaff might be focused on the customer experience at the table, with the quality of the food as a secondary item. They might have separate employees assigned to bus tables, refill drinks, etc. in order to free them up to service the customer. Once again, we hope that this service element is part of the restaurant's competitive advantage.

There is not an inherently correct way to do this as long as it aligns with the competitive advantages of the organization.

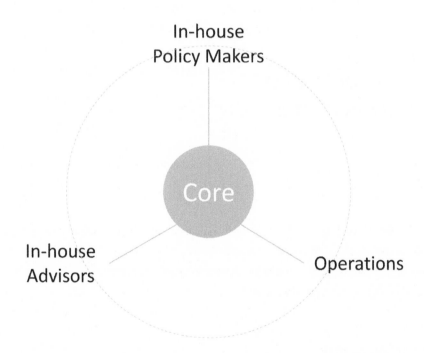

Four (Maybe Five) Coordination Approaches

Once each of the areas within the organization has been categorized into strategy core, in-house advisors, policy makers, and operations, we can turn our attention to how we coordinate employees' work within each group. Every person in a business ultimately ends up in some type of direct-supervision reporting relationship. The goal remains the same: we wish to achieve a situation where we can manage large groups of people with a single manager or leader.

Notwithstanding the fun articles we read in the papers about companies trying out structureless business approaches, the reality is that there are very few, if any, businesses that operate effectively in the long run without some version of a reporting system. Success in strategy implementation is about how to coordinate, evaluate, and manage internal work groups.

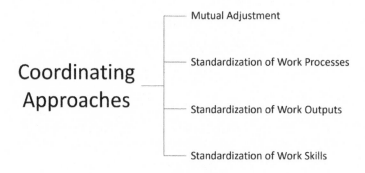

As mentioned before, there are really only four coordinating approaches—we will discuss the potential fifth one separately. The first one on the list gets the closest to the current fad approach of a structureless business, but it operates within a direct supervision structure on some level.

Mutual Adjustment

Mutual adjustment is a coordination approach that puts together a group of people (who ultimately have to report their results to someone) without an internal reporting structure in order to accomplish a task. The approach works best when

- groups are small,

- the need is very well defined,

- the means to answer that need is unknown, or

- the time frame to accomplish the task is very short.

In this approach, there is no one in a supervisory role on the actual team. The team sets the rules, and the team is jointly responsible for the outcome.

This approach has been used quite effectively by "skunk works" groups to find creative solutions to unique problems. The approach was made famous by Lockheed Martin when the organization pulled a group of people together in 1943 to develop a jet fighter. Steve Jobs used the same approach to create the Macintosh. Generally accomplished by separating the group from the hierarchy of the organization, this approach to coordination is extraordinarily effective in very precise circumstances. Time is not taken out for meetings, status reports, budget approvals, etc. The method focuses everyone on a task and works well as long as the aforementioned criteria are well adhered to by the organization.

Mutual adjustment has not been found to work with established departments/ groups within an organization and does not appear to have any value when the group size increases beyond the point where everyone can be in the same area working together. There is something to love about getting virtually 100 percent of employees' time focused on a solution, but the reality is that this coordination approach has limited uses.

Any area where we can utilize mutual adjustment is a bonus. If that approach won't work, then the effort needs to shift to some form of structural standardization still looking to enable employees to focus as much of their energy as possible on the work that needs to be done. The more we can standardize the coordination approach, the more people that can be effectively coordinated under a single manager. There is no particular order to which approach works best or should be considered first. However, I generally start by looking at processes, then move to skills, and finally resort to outputs.

Standardization of Work Processes

When a new organization starts out, everything that happens is a new experience for the employees and the organization as a whole. There is no "organization memory" and no real processes for handling the operations of the organization. I worked with a client that had grown to over $10 million in sales and yet did not have a standard onboarding process for new clients (not a good thing). Virtually the only way for an organization to achieve any real size is for it to standardize processes wherever possible so that the mental firepower of employees can be reserved for unusual situations.

Every aspect of the standard operating elements (orthodox) of an organization should be considered a candidate for a process approach, as can some aspects of every part of the organization. The goal of this approach is for managers to direct and evaluate adherence to the process.

Once the engineers have designed the machinery and flow for cigarettes to be made in a plant, the small number of employees required to run that machinery are there to ensure that the process works as designed. The plant management can and should focus on the processes. As long as the employees are adhering to the processes, all should work well. We certainly look for employees to recommend improvements and inform management when something is not working as planned, but fundamentally, the management team is there to ensure that the processes are being followed. Don't take this the wrong way, but it does not really matter who the actual employee is at each part of the process.

I've seen processes in virtually every aspect of companies. The factory or plant setting is obvious, as are areas of insurance companies that process new applications, paralegals handling real estate closings, waitstaff at most restaurants, residential lawncare teams, dry cleaners, the towel-drying crews at full-service car washes, and so on. Every organization has vast aspects that can be controlled by processes and procedures. We want to organize those into logical groups so that managers and leaders in those areas can coordinate the work of dozens or hundreds of employees at a time. The question constantly asked with this coordination approach is, "Is the employee effectively following the process or procedure that is in place?" If they are, then we move on to the next employee. If they are not, then we council them on the correct process or procedure.

Standardization of Work Skills

When mutual adjustment is not appropriate and the work of the employees simply defies standardization of the processes, then we look to see if there is a group or set of groups that can be managed based on their certified skill set. While there are a lot of both formal and informal skill sets, the only skill sets that matter with this coordination approach are those that can be certified by an outside organization. If done well, it provides the opportunity to manage large numbers of employees with very little direct oversight.

Formal skill sets include outside certifications (CPA, MD with passing board exams, JD with passing the bar, AIA, MBA, PhD, dental hygienist, court stenographer, master plumber, auto mechanic certifications, and various Six Sigma certifications are just some). These are designations designed to guarantee that everyone who has earned the certification has a base level of knowledge and common nomenclature consistent among individuals with these designations. These folks can talk to each other using acronyms that shorten the whole process of communication. Furthermore, they tend to have a common code of conduct that one can rely upon. As with process coordination, the effort turns toward the exceptions. We can all recount instances where this trust was violated. Coordinating the work activities by skill set does not absolve the manager of the responsibility to evaluate and correct performance. It does provide a powerful way to manage lots of people.

The big consulting firms like to hire MBAs from a restricted set of schools, so they know exactly what and how their employees have been taught. The consultants are expected to have a set of skills that can be refined, and then the firm can send large numbers of consultants to far-flung companies. The same can be said of CPAs. If every attorney in the office has a JD and has passed the bar exam for that state, then the office can be managed by a single person regardless of its size. We are only concerned with the attorneys who seem to struggle or are not winning cases (or bringing in clients).

While there are also a great number of informal skill sets, it is virtually impossible to coordinate by them. There is no certainty that everyone has the skill set; by being informal, it is not generally codified and is therefore subject to wide interpretation. As new members join the organization, there is a constant group of employees who will have to be managed separately until they have an understanding of the informal skills.

We look for every opportunity to find groups with established, independent certifications that can be organized together with any operation. Within the typical organization, this might include programming, project management, accounting, legal, and perhaps human resources, to name a few.

Standardization of Work Outputs

When all the other approaches fail to be useful, we resort to using output measures as a means of coordination.

This is where we need to pause in our look at structure. Every part of the organization, regardless of how the work is coordinated, must have output measures. We don't simply trust that the groups being managed by processes, skills, or even mutual adjustment are doing a great job. We verify with output measures. *However*, there is a big difference between having output measures to ensure performance and using output measures to actually coordinate work.

We resort to an output standardization when we *know* what the outcomes of the work effort should be but don't know precisely how each employee should ideally reach that outcome. Consider store clerks. They greet you, help you pick out the item or service that you are looking for, process your sale, and wish you a great day. We have all had experiences with folks who do a great job and folks who do a bad job. Some customers want to chat, other customers just want the facts, and others need their hand held along the way. There is no one way to sell in a store, nor will that way satisfy every customer. Customer service centers are another example where we know we want a satisfied customer who doesn't take too long with one of our reps and does not require too many concessions. Yet there are all types of service representative models that work, and work well (not to mention the companies that have turned this area into one of their competitive advantages).

The key to this type of coordination is the crafting of a series of output metrics that will provide guardrails to prevent performance outside the desired overall goals of the leadership team. They have to be designed in such a way that we attain the performance that we are trying to achieve. We want the store clerk to be friendly, but how much time do we want that person to spend with each customer? We want to sell as many items to a single customer as we can, but how far do we push the customer before he or she is "turned off"? We want the stock to remain refreshed and well organized, but not at the cost of making a customer wait at the register. When we are using output measures to coordinate the work, senior management is examining the results of those output measures to infer whether an employee is effective. Thus, in this case, the output measures used to coordinate the work are the same as the output measures used to evaluate the work being done. It is a relatively cruder approach to coordination.

While an organization's sales force would be a classic example of an area where output measures are particularly effective, so would the business analysis area, the on-site child development center, the reception area, and many more. If you can develop an effective way to use processes or skills to manage a group, then you will only need output measures to *evaluate* their effectiveness. If you must move to output as a means of coordination, then you will have to craft an extensive list of measures to *ensure* effectiveness (keeping in mind that mutual adjustment only works in very limited circumstances).

Standardization of Business Norms

At the beginning of this chapter, we stated that there was a fifth means of work coordination that was still being debated. A standardization of business norms suggests that everyone in the organization understands and fully embraces an "organization norm" that acts as a means of worker coordination. This approach to coordination suggests that a well-developed set of "norms" would guide everyone to do precisely what leadership wanted done at the time. This is the focus of the so-called structureless companies.

While this has been seen in some smaller companies where the founder(s) can constantly reiterate and train employees in the norms of the business, it has not been effectively instituted in a larger organization (although some have claimed that they operate this way). Regardless of the approach, desire, or direction of the business, it is very difficult to provide sufficient context to make this approach work effectively. There are so many nuances to every aspect of a position within an organization that would require the constant reinforcing of so-called norms that it becomes impractical except in the most tightly controlled circumstances.

Some companies have brushed close to this approach, but they did so at a significant cost. That cost is probably well worth it in innovative or groundbreaking areas of business. One of the longest-lasting companies to get close to this approach is W. L. Gore (maker of GORE-TEX). There are structures at the organization, including senior management, divisions, and product-focused groups, but they try to keep units under two hundred people so that there can be direct interaction with every member of the team (called "associates" at Gore).[15] It really appears to be operating as a "pod" approach with mutual adjustment. Another large organization that has tried to move in this direction is Zappos. Instituting what is being called a "holacracy," they are attempting to achieve the same thing as W. L. Gore and the promise of moving closer to a standardization of norms. By 2019 the organization structure had devolved into three hundred "circles" that are arranged hierarchically with headcount and budget controls from the leadership.[16]

The hope and promise of this approach are probably not in its pure implementation, but in the effort to reduce layers of management, speed up decision making, and improve contact with the customer. All of those are laudable goals that don't require experimentation with coordination approaches or the risking of the future of the organization to achieve.

All of these elements (the three areas of the business and the coordinating method utilized) are then put into a structure form that makes sense to the executive management. These structural forms were briefly mentioned at the beginning of the chapter (functional, geographic, global, matrix, multidomestic, etc.) in order to keep the organization focused on doing the standard elements of the business well while expanding the competitive advantages of the business.

Regardless of the organizational structure that is chosen, the hierarchy of decision processes within the organization should be very clear. We want to eliminate hierarchy, and we also want a clear understanding of the focus of the organization. While all four areas that we have structured are necessary for the success of the organization (core, advice-givers, policymakers, and operations), there must be a priority understanding within the organization.

---

15   Garry Hamel, "Innovation Democracy: W. L. Gore's Original Management Model," *Management Information Exchange*, September 23, 2010, http://www.managementexchange.com/story/innovation-democracy-wl-gores-original-management-model.

16   J. Bell, "Exclusive: Zappos Is Looking Beyond E-Commerce to Ensure It Lasts for 1,000 Years," Footwear News, May 6, 2019, https://footwearnews.com/2019/business/retail/zappos-culture-retail-future-strategy-interview-1202777453/.

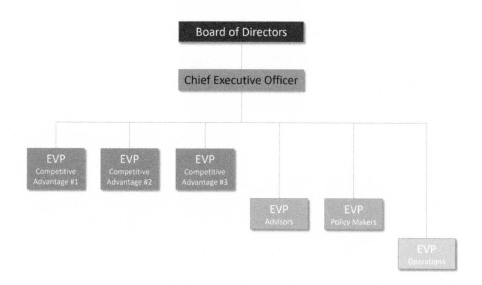

Chapter 10

The Perfect Customer

At this point, we need to cycle back to our discussion about the customer that was started back in chapter 3. In that chapter we simply looked at who the perfect customer appeared to be for the organization as it stood before any real strategy analysis was completed. Just to reiterate, the perfect customer is one who instantly gets the value proposition of the offering and is willing to pay for it. All organizations that have been in existence for any length of time have a set of perfect customers (along with a large set of not-so-perfect customers that cost increasingly more to satisfy as they move away from the value proposition).

Once we have designed a set of competitive advantages for the organization (some current and some that we are developing), it is important to revisit who the perfect customer could be! Which customers would benefit the most from what we now know are our *real* competitive advantages?

There are many approaches to this. A strategy approach is aimed at improving the success rate of the sales team. If you calculate how many customers a typical salesperson can truly pitch to in a week, you realize that there is no way to get to all the potential customers in any reasonable time period. Given that, we want to improve the success rate of those pitches. A sales pitch has a much higher potential for success when made to a customer who truly values our unique competitive advantages.

The second aspect of this effort is to translate that into very observable criteria so our sales team can find those customers. The organization must have a clear, well-understood, and well-communicated idea of who the perfect customer is and how we will find them.

Imagine the following organization:

A manufacturer of braking systems for large vehicle fleets has two plants based in Arkansas. The plants are both relatively old, but the equipment and layout inside is clean with very new equipment.

Competitive advantages include the following:

patented materials that do not separate under stress

(something they currently have that has been a differentiator)

internet-based system to detect brake wear patterns

(something they currently have, but they have not really pushed it with customers and only have it available on one of their more than two hundred plus braking systems)

guaranteed delivery within twenty-four hours of order

(something that they do not do now but have decided would be a real RBA)

The sales team loves what they sell and comes up with their perfect customer:

1. orders a large number of braking systems every month

2. pays on time

3. only buys braking systems from this company

4. wants to save money

5. doesn't use Request for Proposals (RFP) for bidding

6. cares about their employees

THE STRATEGY MINDSET 2.0

7.   needs brakes immediately

8.   is close to this company's manufacturing sites

All of it looks good to the salespeople (and perhaps to everyone in the organization); the only real problem is that it does not help them locate these customers:

orders a large number of braking systems every month

(must have a lot of trucks—this we can find)

pays on time

(Could do a search of financial records on sites like Dunn & Bradstreet)

only buys braking systems from this company

(hmmm...ask them? And how does that help with obtaining new customers?)

wants to save money

(OK...name the company that does not want to save money on something as orthodox as brakes)

doesn't use RFPs for bidding

(sounds good—or bad—but no way to know upfront, and what would you do with the information?)

cares about their employees

(hmmm...)

needs brakes immediately

(seems to exactly counter the first desire)

is close to the company's manufacturing sites

(would make the twenty-four-hour delivery easier, and this is something we can find)

The sales team needs to focus on precisely which customers would benefit most from this company's particular competitive advantages. Given that those advantages are patented materials that do not separate under stress, an internet-based system to detect brake wear patterns, and guaranteed delivery within twenty-four hours of order, a more precise approach to the perfect customer might look something like the following:

truck fleet owners with high stress runs (e.g., mining companies, trucking companies operating in the Rocky Mountain states, and trucking companies operating in the most congested cities)

truck fleet owners who utilize digital tracking (examine websites for companies that pitch digital tracking to their customers—this shows an inclination to automate and make things more efficient)

truck fleet owners who focus on long-haul service (those companies that cannot physically see the truck every day might be more open to an internet-based system of tracking. Also, they might be much more interested in quick delivery of brakes to remote locations)

truck fleet owners with operations in multiple states (check the websites for terminal locations. The more they have, the more they might appreciated the direct delivery without having to maintain inventory. This is especially true if the truck fleet operator has smaller terminals)

The group should take some effort to develop a very specific set of observable criteria that can be used to locate customers who are most likely to value the company's *real* competitive advantages.

Chapter 11

Alignment and the One-Page Strategy Implementation Map

B ringing everything together into a workable strategic plan has been an issue since the birth of management as a field of study. Regardless of how the strategy of the business was developed, communicating that to every employee in a manner that is continually reinforced is quite difficult. Strategic plans earned their classic bad name from the fact that they

- had little to do with the actual operation of the business,

- were never reviewed by senior management after being put into place,

- were ponderous documents bound in huge three-ring binders,

- wasted untold hours of time in their development, and

- often were little more than incremental works that were primarily used for budget purposes.

None of that is strategy, and it is certainly not the way to implement strategy.

Various attempts have been made to rectify this situation. Some companies mandated that their plans be limited in size, causing all kinds of consternation and eight-point font reports by lower-level managers worried about being held account-able without being able to explain the details. Approaches like the balanced scorecard came and went (or should have done so were it not for the hold-out consulting com-panies trying to keep the approach alive), leaving more of a bad taste than actually ac-complishing anything of value. The concepts around the balanced scorecard were fine; the form was ineffective. Thinking about strategy is good, designing a real strategy is better, and actually implementing that strategy is amazing.

The mapping approach to strategy implementation outlined in this chapter has been used quite successfully in many industries and across different-sized operations both in for-profit and nonprofit organizations. It was developed in the early 2000s and allows the entire strategy to be laid out on a single page or screen. If you search the internet for strategy maps, you will see examples of this in various forms. It is very important that you temper your search for these maps due to the fact that the ap-proach has been refined many times over the past two decades. The one used today is far more efficient than the early versions and takes into account the latest thinking in the research field. The sophistication of artistry can be mind-boggling (little avatars climbing ladders). In this chapter, we will look at the fundamentals and a very straight-forward template for doing this within your organization.

A key beginning point to this effort is the decision about how many maps will be needed in the organization. We would prefer to have just *one* map for the entire orga-nization. Unfortunately, the reality is that many companies are too complex for that. While there can and should be an overall map for the whole organization, there will most likely be a need for individual areas to have their own maps.

The best rule of thumb is to create a separate map whenever the competitive set or perfect customer changes significantly. These two elements are the foundation for the strategy that is ultimately implemented. If they differ substantially from group to group within the organization, then each group will need to craft their own strategy map. Therefore, even though we show maps for overall organizations here and in the appendix, recognize that most organizations have many maps that must be tied to-gether into a coherent strategy.

Another key tenet of great strategy implementation is that everyone in the orga-nization understands what the strategy is, how it will be measured (the metrics that you will use), what they can do to impact the strategy, and what the organization will do to support them trying to implement the strategy. Large, convoluted, and difficult

sometimes require more than one conglomerates

to understand "strategies" may look impressive to analysts, but they will not accom-plish the real goal of strategy implementation.

Implementation is accomplished by everyone in the organization. Effective imple-mentation is about fit and alignment within the organization such that the customer receives a consistent experience focused on those elements that truly provide the or-ganization a competitive advantage. The strategy map below (and as seen earlier) has a number of elements:

Header Line

Comparison Set—the list of four or five companies that constitute our compari-son competitive set

Standard Operations (Orthodox)—a list of the two or three big standard ele-ments of the business that are currently substantially below median and will be addressed first

Strategy Map

Comparison Set:
Orthodox:

Unique Differentiators	Customer Experiences (Statements)	Strategic Priorities	Metrics
		What must WE do to Achieve (Project Plans)	

The core part of the map consists of five columns:

Unique Differentiators—Each of the resource-based advantages are listed in this column.

Customer Statements—Each resource-based (competitive) advantage is translated into statements we would like to hear customers say about that element of our offering.

Strategic Priorities—What must be done at the organization level in order to achieve the statements that we have listed in column 2? These will constitute the headlines for the project plans. We list them on the strategy map so that employees know where the major initiatives will be. Generally, we create a project plan for each of the orthodox elements that will be addressed and one for each of the resource-based advantages.

Metrics—What are the activity metrics that will be used by the leadership team to determine whether the organization is moving toward making each of the resource-based advantages the central reason that customers bypass competitors and buy from our organization?

The strategy map is simply a way to bring together all the work from this book into a format that provides guidance to every employee on a daily basis. While the elements of the strategy map are fairly straightforward, it is worth examining the individual elements.

Unique Differentiators

Let's start with the core part of the map. The current or new resource-based advantages (RBA) should be listed in the first column. A key to doing this well is to craft the RBA into a succinct but meaningful set of words. If we go back to the fast-food restaurant we discussed in Chapter 9, you might remember that the two RBAs were as follows:

1. a 24-7 operation where the customer can have breakfast or regular food items anytime, and

2. a private dining area where no cell phone may be used, and no talking is allowed.

We might recraft these into differentiators that state the following:

1. any food, any time

2. quiet room

The goal is to message the essence of the RBA such that everyone in the organization knows the basic approach.

The problem with short concepts is that they often are not sufficiently descriptive. The tendency is to craft RBAs such as the following:

1. customer is first

2. widest offering

3. on-time guarantee

4. transformational operations

5. innovative cost management

6. distributed decisions

If something like these exist, the strategy implementation effort must be refined to get underneath these big concepts to what really constitutes the underlying competitive advantages.

Customer Statements

Each of the differentiators listed needs to be expanded so that every employee knows what the executives meant when they crafted the term—we want to reduce variation in the interpretation by employees. A method that has been shown to work very well is to convert these differentiators into statements that we would want customers (or in some cases, competitors) to say about the organization relative to that specific value driver. While there is no perfect statement, we do want something that might actually be said.

For our fictional fast-food restaurant, we might develop stakeholder statements for each value driver that state the following:

1. any food, any time

    a) customer statements

        i. "I love being able to eat breakfast at night."

        ii. "A burger at eight in the morning is just what the doctor ordered."

    b) competitor statements

        i. "It's just too hard to set up lunch food when we are serving breakfast."

        ii. "No one has ever asked us for eggs at midnight."

2. quiet room

    a) customer statements

        i. "Finally, peace and quiet when I have to eat in a hurry."

       ii. "I'm glad that I don't bother anyone now with the calls I have to take during lunch."

   b) competitor statements

       i. "I wouldn't want to offend our customers like that."

       ii. "No one comes here for quiet time."

The goal is to help the employees see more specifically what each competitive advantage is hoping to accomplish. We pitch this to employees as what we desire to hear customers actually say. The employee is then asked what they can do to help make that a reality.

Strategic Priorities

In order for the organization to start moving toward the statements we want to hear from customers and competitors, there are usually a number of overarching organization efforts that must be in place. These are the crucial elements that the organization needs to do if they want to implement their strategy. In our fast-food example, these might be as follows:

1. develop procedures for ensuring that quiet rooms remain quiet

2. build quiet room facilities in each location

3. develop processes and training to deliver all offered food items 24-7

4. change out all menu boards to reflect new offering

5. change supply stock to reflect varying demand for products offered

The strategic priorities column on the strategy map is designed to show employees where the initial focus will be. All of these initiatives will be turned into fully developed project plans that align the organization. Any initiative within the organization must be put into action, or it is just words on a page. The more specific that action, the more likely the employees will make the effort to achieve the results desired.

Project plans can take a variety of forms and are the subject of many books on the market. There are dozens of approaches online that may be used and many individuals who have earned their PMP (Project Management Professional) designation as experts in project planning.

The three most common approaches are the classic "waterfall" project plan, Hoshin Kanri, and Agile. (or some variation of Agile). Each has their proponents and detractors. I have found that while Agile works well in fast-paced operational areas, it is not well suited for managing an organization, and its performance is virtually impossible for a board of directors to track. Both Hoshin Kanri and waterfall plans are well suited for organization management.

Over the years, I have crafted a waterfall project plan that is simple to use, easy to follow, and easy to put together on any spreadsheet program. There is one project plan for each of the competitive advantages and one for each of the orthodox items that will be addressed first (according to the strategy map).

While these plans can run hundreds of lines long depending upon the complexity of the project, the goal is to maintain a visual on what needs to be completed, what has been completed, and when leadership can expect to hit certain milestones.

One should also note the change in the measures on a project plan as compared to a strategy map. The measure on a project plan should be the visible results of that particular action item being completed. In my estimation, every action item should have a visible outcome. It does me no good for one of my analysts to tell me that they have examined the competitive environment if they have not produced something that can be read by others.

Not going to hit completion date

Team concerned about hitting completion date

On Track

Completed Key Action Item

Key Action Items	Responsible Person (s)	Metrics - Measure(s) of Success	Start Date	Completion Date	Status (red, yellow, green)	Status Update

Metrics

As we covered extensively in chapter 8, the development of strategy metrics is a crucial part of the implementation process. We want to know what actions we expect employees to do before we implement a strategy. The metrics need to be specific to the element (differentiator and statement) being evaluated.

There is a big difference between the metrics used in a strategy map and those used to measure the overall performance of the organization (or part of the organization covered by the map). While we want to know how the overall organization is performing (ROI, net profit margin, free cash flow, market share, etc.), in the strategy map, we are trying to evaluate *activities* so we can be sure that the strategy itself is being implemented. If we are right about the direction of the strategy, *and* it is actually being implemented (no small feat), then the organization performance measures should move up post hoc (viewing and analyzing the data after the effort has been expended).

In this instance, the strategy map measures might include the following:

1. number of locations with quiet rooms divided by total number of locations (we want this to go up)

2. number of minutes before an employee addressed a noise complaint / measured weekly - we want this to go down

3. number of minutes between checks to ensure quiet rooms remain quiet rooms / measured store to store and weekly - we want this to go down

4. number of seconds to deliver breakfast items sold outside the time frame of 6:00 a.m. to 10:30 a.m. divided by number of seconds to deliver lunch items sold during same time period (we would like to see this equal 1)

Each of these measures is geared toward measuring employee actions that senior management believes will directly impact the competitive advantage that the organization is trying to focus on. Although there will be some lag effect, we would like to see all the classic financial measures of performance increase as well.

Life is good when the financial measures of performance increase as our strategy (activity) metrics move in the desired directions. We can be confident that the strategy is effective.

The strategy is flawed when we see the financial measures of performance decrease as our strategy (activity) metrics move in the desired directions. The strategy is being implemented by the employees, but it is not having a positive effect on our overall performance. We are spending time, energy, and resources and not getting a gain.

The strategy is not being implemented if we see the strategy metrics not moving in the desired direction, whether or not financial measures of performance increase or decrease. Changes in financial performance are simply a result of random events and activities that are not being coordinated.

The overall strategy map outlines the key competitive advantages of the organization. Converting that into an operational plan is an important step. Conceptually, we view the process as the following chart illustrates.

Chapter 12

Nonprofit Organizations

Although virtually everything that has been discussed in this book about strategy design and strategy implementation applies to both for-profit and nonprofit organizations, the reality is that there are some differences in the approach and design that make nonprofit organizations unique. I examine each of the nuances to the model below.

Customers. While all nonprofits have clients whom they serve (and are the reason for their existence), these are not the "customers" of the organization from a strategy perspective. The customer is the one who parts with their money and/or time to support the nonprofit. This means that the nonprofit must have a set of compelling competitive advantages with how they address their clients' needs such that donors, volunteers, grant organizations, government agencies, and the like will go past the other nonprofits and come to that nonprofit.

This means that the strategy map must be geared toward attracting those customers so that the nonprofit has the resources to do the most good it can do.

Competitors. Nonprofits do indeed have competitors. They compete for donation dollars, volunteers, access to grants, recognition by government officials, and recognition by the client who would most benefit from the offering of the nonprofit. There are many nonprofits that provide similar services to similar groups of clients.

I have worked with dozens of nonprofit organizations that feed homeless people. There are a vast number of approaches to the issue of hunger in general and specifically how it is handled within the homeless population of a particular area. What makes the approach that one particular nonprofit uses a competitive advantage? Why should donors and volunteers provide resources and time to one over another? What is the best way to deal with hunger in the homeless population?

Mission/vision/purpose. Unlike with a classic for-profit organization, we generally do not develop the mission of a nonprofit from the competitive advantages. The mission of most nonprofits is established around their mandate for the client community. While we still want it to be short, simple, etc., the board of directors generally establishes the mission and vision together in order to inspire those who work at the organization.

Many (certainly not all) employees at nonprofits are there partly due to calling and partly for a job. The pay and benefits at many are less than those at for-profit businesses in the area, and thus employees must really want to be a part of the nonprofit. That is generally described in the mission and/or vision of the organization. "End Homelessness as we know it," "Every person has a full meal every day," "Inspire greatness," "Employ the greatest number of challenged individuals in meaningful employment," and the list goes on.

As most nonprofits' boards of directors are made up of volunteers from whom they hope to receive sizable donations of money and time, the mission/vision/purpose is also directed at attracting them.

Strategy map. Most of the elements remain the same; however, the statements differ a bit from those of for-profit businesses. In nonprofits, we like to consider how what we believe is a real RBA might be seen from a donor, client, volunteer, and even government group. It is much more of a stakeholder approach to strategy.

Let's take a look at an example map from a nonprofit organization.

Non-Profit Example Strategy Map

Comparison Set: Other Non-Profits interacting with the same client community in your area
Orthodox to Median: Technology | Professional Development | Standardization

Unique Differentiators	Client / Donor / Volunteer Experiences (Statements)	Project Plans	Metrics
We Come To You	**Client** "My counselor will meet me anywhere" **Client** "I'd know my counselor anywhere"		➢ Visits outside office / Total Visits ➢ Staff Time Face-to-Face / Total Time
Comprehensive Center of Care	**Client** "I got more help than I expected" **Donor** "I didn't know you could do so much in just one day" **Community** "I know X has the ability to provide the help needed"		➢ # of clients who are personally introduced to more than one service / total clients ➢ # of 'Needs' satisfied same day as visit / Total # of clients seen in a day ➢ # of INTERNAL referrals / clients per month

In this example, the nonprofit would have listed which other nonprofits or even for-profit organizations are working with clients on similar needs. In the "Orthodox to Median" line, this particular nonprofit was having issues with technology (they were using old PCs and running in an unsecure environment with lots of personal information), professional development (the organization hired very talented people but did little to help them keep up with changes in the industry), and standardization (this particular nonprofit really dealt with every client as a brand-new case with no standard method for on-boarding the client, collecting information, or setting expectations). All three were well below the standard expectations established by other nonprofits in the immediate area.

The two areas where they felt they had real competitive advantages relative to the other nonprofits was their counselors approach to meeting clients anywhere they wanted (as opposed to most of the competitors, who required clients to come to them, wait in a lobby, and get called back to the counselor's office) and the vast number of resources that they provided in-house to their client community.

In the statement column, we see that in some cases the statements are strictly from the client, while in another, we get various perspectives on the same competitive advantage. Once again, all of the metrics are designed to be activity metrics that the leadership team would like to see employees strive to improve.

Appendix

Example Maps

It seems valuable to look at a few examples of strategy maps for some organizations. These have been crafted by my students in various executive classes for real companies as a way of applying the technique outside their own organizations (it's safer that way). The students had no contact with the real companies, and these were completed with only publicly available information. They are not from the actual companies, and any actual resemblance to the strategies being considered by those companies would be coincidence. Unfortunately, I am not able to provide the actual strategy maps of my clients for obvious reasons. I've modified these maps in order to make them more applicable to the reader.

In each case, I've made notes about what would improve the effort.

Dunkin'

Strategy Map   DUNKIN'

Comparison Set: Krispy Kreme | Tim Horton | McDonalds | Starbucks | Panera
Orthodox to Median: Unknown

Value Drivers	Customer Statements	Metrics
Pace of Menu Innovation	"I go to Dunkin' because they always have fresh new food items" "No matter where I travel, I can find something fun to try at the local Dunkin'"	# new ideas pitched to culinary team per month # recipes created / # ideas pitched to culinary team # in-store visits to pitch LTO products / # stores
Localized Experience at Scale	"My local Dunkin' store is always offering a promotion when there's an event in the community." "Dunkin' stores are a part of my local community – I even know the owners!"	# local events attended by franchise owners, per quarter # dollars allocated to public community-facing events / total amount included in local advertising fund
On-The-Run	"I never worry about missing a meeting when I go to Dunkin'"	# hand-held food items / total food offerings # mobile enhancements aimed at reducing transaction time / total # tickets # stores redesigned to speed up sales / # total stores

This strategy map lays out three resource-based advantages that the group believes Dunkin' had in 2019 over the competition. They list the competitive set as they saw it but did not address standard operations (orthodox expectations) that they felt were below median. It is actually quite difficult to evaluate these standard operations from outside the organization. It requires in-depth knowledge about the company except in the most visible and egregious cases.

The group did a very good job with the activity metrics. Each is focused on activities under the control of the employees, and each appears to be directly aimed at the competitive advantage listed. They do not list the big project plans on this map.

Lowe's

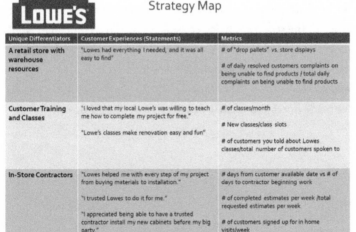

Unique Differentiators	Customer Experiences (Statements)	Metrics
A retail store with warehouse resources	"Lowes had everything I needed, and it was all easy to find"	# of "drop pallets" vs. store displays # of daily resolved customers complaints on being unable to find products / total daily complaints on being unable to find products
Customer Training and Classes	"I loved that my local Lowe's was willing to teach me how to complete my project for free." "Lowe's classes make renovation easy and fun"	# of classes/month # New classes/class slots # of customers you told about Lowes classes/total number of customers spoken to
In-Store Contractors	"Lowes helped me with every step of my project from buying materials to installation." "I trusted Lowes to do it for me." "I appreciated being able to have a trusted contractor install my new cabinets before my big party."	# days from customer available date vs # of days to contractor beginning work # of completed estimates per week /total requested estimates per week # of customers signed up for in home visits/week

Strategy Map

Competitive Set:
- Home Depot
- Menard's
- Ace Hardware
- True Value

Orthodox in:
- Large number of products
- Online presence
- Carry major brands
- Customer service

In this strategy map suggested for Lowe's Home Improvement, the team laid out the competitive set and orthodox elements to address on the right-hand side. The first orthodox element seems to suggest that the Lowe's needs to reduce the number of products they carry, and yet the first competitive advantage seems to reward a large selection. In this case, the team felt that the other three orthodox elements were so visibly below the median expectation that they could list them.

Some of the metrics (certainly one of the toughest parts of a strategy map to get right) would cause me concern if I were in the leadership at Lowe's. The second metric for the second competitive advantage seems to reward the almost constant creation of new classes. New classes are great, but there is a lot of value provided by repeat classes on popular projects/subjects. Not only does the class get better over time as it is refined, but there is an almost constant demand for the basics.

The metrics for the third competitive advantage has a number of problems that point out the need for real precision on the part of the leadership team. The first metric is about speed, but there is nothing about speed in any of the statements. The exact same issue comes up again with the second metric. It is also about speed. The third metric is not an activity metric. Note that it does not measure activities that employees could perform to get the organization closer to the statements desired. Instead it is an outcome metric—it is a good outcome metric and one we would want to see, but we need to be clear about what activities we believe employees should perform so that this outcome metric goes up.

Papa John's

Orthodox Measures: Hot pizza at delivery, order correctness
Competitive Set: Pizza Hut | Dominos | Little Caesars | Mellow Mushroom | Marco's Pizza

Unique Differentiators	Customer Statements	Strategic Plans	Metrics
Dependable Taste	*Consumer:* "I know exactly what I'm getting every time I order from Papa John's." *Franchisee:* "I save a lot of time having a one-stop shop to order everything and feel confident the quality will be top-notch."	Deliver as Fresh from the Oven Match Industry for Order Correctness	# of stores using QC / total # of stores # of ingredients through QC center / total ingredients
Late Night Availability	*Consumer:* "Papa John's is the only pizza chain up as late as I am." *Consumer:* "Papa John's delivery time is the same whether I order at 5 PM or 3 AM."	Worldwide consistency in ingredients / design Develop the 24-hour Pizza Chain	# nights open past 4am / 365 (by store – weekly) # of deliveries on time after 12am / # of deliveries after 12am
Omni-Channel Presence	*Consumer:* "I love that I can get my favorite Papa John's pizza via delivery, food truck, or grocery store." *Consumer:* "I stop by the food truck on my way home from the bar because it's faster than getting a pizza delivered."	Papa John's EVERYWHERE you want a Pizza	# menu items available in omni-channel / total # of pre-fixed menu items # pizzas ready at order / total # of pizzas sold

Papa John's has been an interesting business to watch, as it almost imploded and is now trying to reset itself in a crowded industry. This is a very interesting strategy map, as it fits the classic model that we see with many organizations. As stated earlier in this book, it is very common to find one real, current competitive advantage at an organization. In this case, it is the first one, according to the students and their analysis: dependable taste. The second competitive advantage is something new for the organization but not a huge leap, as there are franchises now that are staying open very late. The third competitive advantage is completely new. The recommendation is to create food trucks, sell in grocery stores, and make Papa John's pizza available everywhere and anytime.

The metrics are a bit difficult to follow at times but were well explained by the team. Note that in this map, the team added in five project plans for the business to organize around: one each for the two orthodox issues that the team felt were below median (hot pizza delivery and order correctness) as well as three focused on the competitive advantages pitched (dependable taste, late-night availability, and an Omni-channel presence).

Charles E. Bamford, PhD

D r. Chuck Bamford is the managing partner at Bamford Associates, LLC, a strategy consulting firm founded in 2013 that is focused on the *design* and *implementation* of a compelling set of competitive advantages.

Dr. Bamford led both M&A and corporate training groups for twelve years prior to pursuing his PhD. He is the author of *The Strategy Mindset* as well as two of the market leading strategy and entrepreneurship textbooks used in both undergraduate and graduate programs around the world (15th edition, Pearson, and 3rd edition, McGraw-Hill, respectively).

 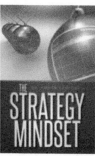  

Chuck is a regular speaker at conferences, trade shows, corporate events, and conventions. He is also the author of the fiction novel *Some Things are Never Forgiven*.

Chuck has published eighteen research articles in the top-referred academic journals in the fields of strategy and entrepreneurship.

Dr. Bamford is an adjunct (part-time) professor of strategy at Duke University (Fuqua) and the University of Notre Dame (Mendoza). He has taught at universities in Scotland, Hungary, and the Czech Republic. He was previously a professor at the University of Richmond, Texas Christian University, and Tulane University, among others. Over the past twenty-five years, he has been honored with *twenty-two* Professor of the Year awards, including *twelve* Executive MBA Professor of the Year awards. He was named a Noble Foundation Fellow in *Teaching Excellence* and a *Poets & Quants* Favorite Professor.

Chuck earned his BS at the University of Virginia (McIntire School of Commerce), an MBA at Virginia Tech (finance) and a PhD in strategy and entrepreneurship at the University of Tennessee.

Made in the USA
Las Vegas, NV
07 April 2021

20990283R00114